Becoming A True Christian

Pastor Myron L. Philippi

Faithful Life Publishers
North Fort Myers, FL

This book is a guide to evangelize
those who do not know the Lord Jesus Christ
as their personal Savior.

These lessons can be used in an individual
Bible study or in classes with others to help
them to become true Christians.

Also, this book is often used as a fundamental
orientation for the spiritual growth of a
true Christian.

FIRST PRINTING in Spanish - December 1995 - 2,300 books
SECOND EDITION revised in Spanish - March 1997 - 3,250 books
THIRD EDITION revised in Spanish - April 2001 - 4,500 books
FOURTH EDITION revised in Spanish - May 2003 - 10,500 books
FIFTH EDITION revised in Spanish - October 2007 - 4,500 books
SIXTH EDITION revised in Spanish - May 2012 - 3,070 books

FIRST PRINTING in English - October 1997 - 4,200 books
SECOND REVISION in English - January 2005 - 4,500 books
THIRD REVISION in English - January 2007 - 6,500 books
FOURTH REVISION in English - April 2013 - 3,200 books

FIRST PRINTING in Russian - January 2007 - 5000 books

****
Address where you can request more books or spiritual help:

Pastor Myron L. Philippi
6465 99th Way N. #17-B
St. Petersburg, FL 33708
727-393-7846
E-mail: philippi@becoming-a-christian.org
Web: www.becoming-a-christian.org

Mission Organization:
Baptist World Mission
P. O. Box 2149
Decatur, AL 35602
256-353-2221

Scripture quotations are from the Authorized King James Version of the Holy Bible.

ISBN: 978-1-937129-67-5
Faithful Life Publishers • 3335 Galaxy Way • North Fort Myers, FL 33903
www.faithfullifepublishers.com   info@FaithfulLifePublishers.com

Art work: D.G. José Orozco Rodriguez, Tel: 52-333-344-0903 Guadalajara, MX

Printed in the United States of America

18 17 16 15 14 13   4 5 6 7 8 9 10

Dedication

I dedicate this new revision of ***Becoming a True Christian***
to all missionaries and pastors around the world who
are faithfully teaching and preaching the sound doctrine
of the Gospel of our Lord and Savior Jesus Christ.
Please take very seriously 2nd Timothy 2:1-3 where the
Apostle Paul gives us a great admonition:
Thou therefore, my son, be strong in the grace that is in
Christ Jesus. And the things that thou hast heard of me
among many witnesses, the same commit thou to
faithful men, who shall be able to teach others also.
Thou therefore endure hardness, as a good soldier of Jesus Christ.
I trust all of your expectations will be surpassed
as you use this book in your ministry. Our prayer to God is
that through this study of the Word of God you
will be encouraged to do your best to serve
our Lord Jesus Christ with a relentless strength
that only comes from Him.

Your servant in Christ,

Pastor Myron L. Philippi

Important Recommendations from Pastors, Missionaries & Layman

Becoming A True Christian is an excellent Bible study book, which takes a lost person through a series of studies on sin, repentance, salvation, and basic discipleship. Learn what it means to really be a Christian through these lessons. This book should be place in the hands of Christians to encourage them to begin Bible studies with the unsaved. These lessons will help ground Christians in the Word of God and will help motivate them to be soul winners. It, also, will deepen the Christian's awareness for the need for sound doctrine.

Pastor Gordon Sears
Song Fest • Coldwater, Michigan

We use *Becoming a True Christian* in our churches in Ensenada, Mexico, for Bible studies with both saved and unsaved people. We use this book with the lost, because it presents the Gospel in a thorough, but easy-to-understand manner for all ages. They can really comprehend their lost condition, repent of their sin, and give themselves to the Lord Jesus Christ, so that they can be truly saved. We use this book with the saved, to disciple them, and to be sure that they truly understand the Christian life. I strongly recommend *Becoming a True Christian* for home Bible studies to be promoted in all churches.

Pastor Donald Holmes
Missionary, Baptist World Mission • Ensenada, Baja California, Norte, Mexico

I heartily recommend this book for use either in your personal Bible Study, for Sunday School classes, or for teaching an entire church this true and effective method of "soul winning." This book is being used for one-on-one Bible studies with lost sinners and also for biblical follow-up with those who have been converted to Jesus Christ! The careful and prayerful study of the lessons in *Becoming a True Christian* with a lost soul will usually result in the person coming under great conviction and be marvelously saved or, as happens with some, they discontinue the Bible study. I give *Becoming a True Christian* to all of my clients, and seek to have a Bible study class with them.

Sherman C. Weeks
Licensed Public Accountant, Londonderry, NH

Pastor Myron Philippi's book, *Becoming a True Christian,* is powerful for at least two reasons: 1) It is biblical, placing a strong emphasis upon the sinfulness of man and the need for repentance in salvation, 2) because it is biblical, it results in genuine converts to Christ as opposed to the shallow, artificial decisions so common today. This book produces fruit that remains because it appropriately uses THE BOOK, the Word of God. Our church uses this book for evangelism and we recommend it for all Bible believing churches.

Pastor Bruce Hamilton
Senor Pastor of the Hamilton Acres Baptist Church, Fairbanks, AK

Table of Contents

Preface

This book was written because of the great necessity for adequate material to put in the hands of Christians to encourage them to begin Bible studies with the unsaved. It is a helpful Scriptural guide they can use to show others how to become a Christian and be truly transformed by the grace of God. In our church in Guadalajara, Mexico, even new Christians enthusiastically accept the challenge to hold a one-on-one Bible class and share what they have learned, using this book. Our prayer is that God may use these lessons to ground Christians in the Word of God and motivate them to be soul winners. This book can also help deepen the Christian's awareness of the need for sound doctrine.

A farmer is a steward of the ground. He is responsible to be careful so that it will produce in the future. Likewise, pastors and teachers of the Gospel are also stewards of the ground where the Word of God is sown. We all are responsible to the Lord Jesus Christ for what we do in preparing the ground so that it will produce true spiritual fruit in the future. The Word of God needs to be carefully planted in the hearts of individuals so that they will understand. *Thou therefore, my son, be strong in the grace that is in Christ Jesus. And the things that thou hast heard of me among many witnesses, the same commit thou to faithful men, who shall be able to teach others also.* (2nd Timothy 2:1-2)

We give thanks to God for the ideas and suggestions that have come to me through pastors, missionaries, and teachers of the Word of God. Their suggestions have made it possible to place a more complete book in your hands and to enable you to teach others also.

Pastor Myron L. Philippi

Foreword

Pastor Myron Philippi has served for over five decades as a missionary evangelist, discipler and church planter, ministering in Venezuela, the United States and Mexico. He is well-equipped to write on the subject that has dominated his life's service to Christ.

This book is an English translation and update of his original Spanish Bible study course, *Llegando A Ser Un Verdadero Cristiano*. It is solidly biblical in its presentation and has been tested and proven in the laboratory of missionary church-planting experience. As you work through the text of this book, you will be impressed with how much of the Word of God is woven into its fabric.

Pastor Philippi's burden for a biblical gospel and his zeal in seeking to make genuine disciples of Jesus Christ is a spiritual quality that should characterize every servant of Christ. It is my delight to recommend this volume to you for use in working with individuals and groups in bringing them to understand what it means to become a true Christian.

Dr. Bud Steadman

Executive Director, Baptist World Mission • Decatur, Alabama

Welcome Student

We greet you in the name of our Lord and Savior Jesus Christ. We are thankful that you are taking time to study God's Word. We want to encourage you to make this a priority in your life as you study the lessons faithfully and fill in the blanks, asking God to guide you and help you understand His Word as you look up every Scripture. Each student should be encourage to have his own book and we suggest that you use a pencil to enable you to make corrections when necessary.

Study carefully and be diligent. Do not let other things crowd out your desire to study God's Word. We all need to come to Christ Jesus for He is the only *way, the truth and the life.* (John 14:6) The way of salvation is clearly presented in the Word of God in order that we might truly be born again by the Spirit of God and receive His true salvation.

In Matthew 7:13, Christ Jesus contrasts two ways and two destinies; one way leads to life, and the other leads to eternal destruction. This is a clear warning that God gives to us, and we must make a choice. This is the most important decision of your life. God desires to bring you into a wonderful personal relationship with Himself through His Son, Christ Jesus. It is our sincere desire that He will become your personal Savior.

But these are written, that ye might believe that Jesus is the Christ, the Son of God; and that believing ye might have life through His name. (John 20:31)

May God richly bless you as you study His Word.

Pastor Myron L. Philippi

Chapter One

The True Christian

Therefore if any man be in Christ, he is a new creature:
old things are passed away; behold,
all things are become new.
2nd Corinthians 5:17

WHAT IS A TRUE CHRISTIAN?

Many false and erroneous ideas exist concerning how one can really become a true Christian. It is imperative to understand how to be saved according to the Word of God. Romans 10:17 declares, *So then faith cometh by _____, and hearing by the Word of God.* The plan of God to save the sinner is not a simple plan for salvation designed by man, but the perfect plan given by God from the foundation of the world.

It is important to understand that the plan of salvation which God has presented in His Word is completely based upon His great love for all mankind. Everything is clearly presented with accuracy in the Bible. We must carefully follow God's instructions. True salvation, which is of God, does not come through good works, neither by making great personal sacrifices through rites, laws, education, riches or by living a moral life. It is only through the grace of God that we can become a "new creation" in Christ Jesus.

I. THE FIRST CHRISTIANS

1. Throughout the Bible the term *disciple* is used not only for the true believer, but also in making reference to those who showed interest in the Gospel as seen in John 6:60-66. It is important to make this distinction. Besides being called disciples, by what name were the followers of Jesus Christ first known? (Read Acts 9:1-2; 19:9,23; 24:14) **Please underline the correct answer.**
(Believers)   (Those of the Way)   (Christians)

2. Jesus Christ said in John 14:6, *I am the* _____, *the truth, and the life: no man cometh unto the Father, but by me.* This truth prevailed throughout His messages and ministry.

3. Where were the disciples of Jesus Christ first called *Christians?* (Acts 11:25-26) _____. The name *Christian* means– "Christ-ones or the followers of Christ." It is a direct personal identification with the Lord Jesus Christ.

II. THOSE WHO APPEAR TO BE CHRISTIANS

The fact that someone teaches or preaches, casts out demons or performs miracles in the name of Jesus Christ is not proof that he is a servant of God. **Read carefully Matthew 7:21-23 to answer the following questions:**

1. List three things these people claimed to have done in the name of Jesus Christ.

   a. _____
   b. _____
   c. _____

2. Because they used the name of Jesus saying, *Lord, Lord*, did these people consider themselves to be Christians? _____

3. Were they true Christians? _____ Why? (Matthew 7:23) _____
   _____
   _____
   _____
   _____
   _____

2

4. In Matthew 7:22-23 what were the people relying on in order to enter Heaven? **Please place a circle around the letter that best describes what <u>they</u> believed.**

   a. They had trusted only in Jesus Christ as their Savior, having repented of their sins with all their heart and given themselves to Him.

   b. They relied on certain accomplishments and works that they had done in the name of the Lord Jesus Christ in order to be saved.

   c. They trusted in their religion, because they felt that it was the best, and it was what their parents had taught them.

5. If a person has the capacity to preach, prophesy the future, cast out demons or do miracles in the name of Jesus Christ, is this proof that he is a true Christian and that he really belongs to Jesus Christ? _____ Why? _____

   _____

6. Since they did not do these things in the power of God, of who are they ministers? (2nd Corinthians 11:14-15) _____

   _____

7. Who will enter into Heaven according to Matthew 7:21? _____

   _____

8. After reading the Gospels we understand that Jesus chose twelve men, called apostles, to follow Him in a very special way. Among those twelve was a man by the name of Judas Iscariot, who was a classic example of someone who pretended to be a true follower of Jesus Christ, but lived a life of deception. In John 13:21-22 Jesus said, *Verily, verily, I say unto you, that one of you shall betray me. Then the disciples looked one on another, doubting of whom he spake.* Again Jesus stated in Matthew 26:24-25, *but woe unto that man by whom the Son of man is betrayed! It had been good for that man if he had not been born. Then Judas, which betrayed him, answered and said, Master, is it I?* How was Judas able to deceive those he had been with for years? _____

   _____

   Did Judas Iscariot deceive Jesus Christ? _____

9. Read carefully Acts 8:5-25. Simon, the sorcerer, had believed and was baptized. Was Simon really a true Christian? _____ Simon had never been converted to Jesus Christ. He was just another false "believer." How can we know? _____

_____

III. SAUL'S LIFE BEFORE HIS CONVERSION

The Bible describes the life of Saul of Tarsus, an unusual man who was known by all Jews. Before his conversion he was one of the pharisaical leaders in Judaism and a member of the most important religious organization of that day, the Great Sanhedrin. **Read carefully the history of this renown man in Acts 26:9-12 and Philippians 3:4-6.**

1. What type of a person was Saul before his conversion? (Acts 9:1) _____

_____

2. Before his conversion, Saul felt that there was nothing lacking in his religious life. In Philippians 3:6, what was Saul's attitude toward the church? _____
How did he consider himself? _____.

3. What religion did Saul profess? (Galatians 1:13) _____

4. Did Saul believe in God? (Acts 22:3-4) _____ How did Saul show his fanaticism for his religion? _____

5. What motivated Saul to persecute the followers of Jesus Christ? (Acts 26:4-12; 1st Timothy 1:13) _____

6. Why did Saul believe that it was his responsibility to persecute Christians?

_____

_____

7. Was Saul fanatical or lukewarm in his fervor to defend his religious beliefs? (Acts 22:3-5) _____

8. How do you know that Saul was fanatical? (Galatians 1:13-14) _____

_____

9. Was Saul faithful to his religion? _____

10. Was Saul convinced that his religious beliefs were true? _____

11. Prior to his conversion to Jesus Christ did Saul have a personal relationship with God or was he just religious? _____

12. In what was Saul trusting? (Philippians 3:4) _____
    In this passage, what does the word, "flesh" mean? _____
    _____

13. According to the Word of God, what was lacking in Saul's life? _____
    _____
    _____

14. Can a person believe in God, be fervent in his religion, be very sincere, be convinced that he is in the truth, but at the same time be very wrong and be condemned by God? _____

IV. THE CONVERSION OF SAUL

Read the personal testimony of Saul in Acts 9:1-22 and Acts 22:3-16 to understand how his conversion occurred.

1. What did Saul see that came from above? _____

2. What was his reaction? _____

3. What did Saul hear? _____

4. Who spoke with Saul? (Acts 9:5) _____

5. Where did Saul go after he saw the light and heard the voice of Jesus Christ? _____

6. How many days was Saul blind? _____

7. How many days and nights was Saul fasting because of his sadness for his sinful condition? _____

8. Who looked for Saul in Damascus to tell him how to become a true Christian? _____

9. How do we know that Saul was truly converted to Jesus Christ and did not just have a desire to unite with a new sect or religion? (Acts 9:20)
    _____
    _____

5

10. What are the results of a true conversion that we have seen through studying this lesson? (2nd Corinthians 5:17-18) _____

_____

_____

Saul was convinced that Jesus is God, and not just a common man. In Acts 9:5, 20 and 26:15, he was speaking directly with Jesus Christ. Romans 1:1-4 also confirms this declaration. We are convinced of the fact that Jesus Christ is God through reading the Word of God, the Bible. Throughout John's Gospel, Jesus Christ is presented as God. We find the truth of His Deity in many other passages such as Mark 14:60-64; John 5:1-18; Romans 10:17; Philippians 2:3-11; Titus 2:11-13; Hebrews 1:5-13 and 1st John 5:20.

Study carefully the passage regarding the conversion of Saul in Acts 9:17-19. In a few brief words we are told of Saul's meeting with Ananias and the message God had for Saul. We see that Saul believed, obeyed and later was baptized in water by Ananias. Now read Acts 22:12-16 where there is more information regarding Saul's conversion. Ananias, a servant of the Lord, gave Saul the Gospel message, Saul believed with all his heart and was converted to Jesus Christ.

Later Saul's name was changed to Paul. When the Apostle Paul gave his testimony before the people of Jerusalem regarding his conversion, he told them what Ananias had said: *now why tarriest thou? Arise, and be* _____.

The word *baptism* is mentioned several times in the Bible; however, not all refer to water baptism. The word *baptism* in Greek means – "put into or place into" something or someone. In this passage there is no mention of water, but Ananias tells Saul to place himself **into**, that is, place all his confidence in the Lord Jesus Christ as his personal Savior. This happened when he truly repented of his sin and gave himself to the Lord Jesus Christ with all his heart.

In Acts 22:16 Ananias continued saying, *and wash away thy sins, calling on the name of the Lord.* Saul called upon the Lord Jesus Christ for salvation, and his sins were washed away (forgiven). The only way that a person can have his sins washed away is through the redeeming work of the Lord Jesus Christ. On the cross of Calvary He took upon Himself our sin, received our punishment and died for us. Saul repented of his

6

sin, asked for forgiveness, and put his complete faith and confidence in the Lord Jesus Christ as his Savior. God forgave Saul's sin and from then on Saul's greatest desire was to serve Him with all his heart.

Regrettably, many desire to see lights, hear voices or have an emotional experience in order to have a conversion like Saul's. The way that God received Saul's attention was appropriate for his need; however, God uses many different things to get our attention and bring us to faith in Jesus Christ. God's plan or method of salvation never changes. You must not ignore the fact that the Lord Jesus Christ wants you to be converted to Him. Do you realize this? _____

1. Did Saul receive salvation from the extra bright light that he saw? _____

2. Did the words that Jesus spoke to Saul give him salvation? (Acts 9:4-6) _____

3. Was Saul saved in obedience to the command of Jesus Christ by going to Damascus? _____

4. Did his profound sadness and fasting save him? _____

5. What command did Jesus give to Saul in Acts 9:6? _____
   _____

6. Was Saul converted on the way to Damascus or with Ananias? _____ What factors brought you to that conclusion?
   _____
   _____ The answer is very obvious. Ananias gave the Gospel message to Saul, he understood, he repented of his sin, trusted Jesus Christ as his personal Savior and was converted by giving himself to the Lord Jesus Christ. In that moment Saul was saved and became the property of God.

V. THE LIFE OF SAUL AFTER HIS CONVERSION

Study the commission that Christ gave to Saul in Acts 26:16-20. Jesus Christ gave him the order to go to the Gentiles to preach the Gospel.

1. In what way was Saul changed after his conversion? (verse 20) __
   _____
   _____

2. To what people was Saul sent? _____ (When the name *Gentile* is mentioned in the Bible it refers to "everyone who is not of the Jewish race.")

3. In Acts 26:18 Christ gave the command to Saul *to open their eyes* [to the Truth] *and to turn from darkness to light, and from the power of Satan unto* _____, *that they may receive forgiveness of sins, and inheritance among them which are sanctified* [the saved] *by* _____ *that is in me.* What is the darkness from which we must turn to be converted? _____

4. According to Acts 3:19 and Acts 20:21, how can you receive forgiveness of your sins? _____
   _____
   _____

5. According to 2nd Corinthians 5:17, what are some of the results of a true conversion? _____
   _____

   List several **new things** that occurred in the life of Saul after his conversion. _____
   _____
   _____

VI. WHAT IS A TRUE CHRISTIAN?

Read the following verses: Acts 4:11-12; John 3:3; John 8:31-32, 1st Peter 1:22-23. **Please circle the numbers which best describe a true Christian.**

1. A true Christian is a person that believes in God with all his heart. This means that this person has placed (deposited) all his confidence in the redeeming work that the Lord Jesus Christ did on the cross for him by dying for his sins.

2. A true Christian is one who has studied the Bible under the direction of excellent religious teachers.

3. A true Christian is one who believes in God and tries to do the best that he can by doing many good works in order to gain his salvation.

4. A true Christian is one who was born into a Christian family, is baptized and faithfully follows the traditions of the church.

5. A true Christian is one who recognizes his terrible sinful condition, has repented of his sin and with all of his heart has given himself to the Lord Jesus Christ.

6. A true Christian is one who has repented of his sin, has trusted Christ Jesus as his Savior and has been born again into the family of God. This is not a physical birth but a spiritual one. As true evidence of this salvation there is a transformation in his life.

REVIEW QUESTIONS - CHAPTER 1

THE TRUE CHRISTIAN

1. Are all who consider themselves to be Christians really saved? _____ Why? _____

2. Is it proof that a person belongs to Jesus Christ if he preaches, casts out demons, does miracles or other wonderful things in the name of Jesus? _____ Why? _____

3. If you believe in God, are you assured of a place in Heaven? _____ Why? (James 2:19) _____

4. If you are faithful to your religion and sincerely believe in it, will that save you? _____ Why? (Galatians 2:16) _____
_____

5. Is it possible for you to have the assurance of going to Heaven when you die, even while you are still living? _____ How? _____
_____

6. Are only those saved who have repented of their sins, trusted **only** in Jesus Christ as their personal Savior, and given themselves to Him with all their heart? _____ Explain. _____
_____

7. Can a person become a Christian by doing good works? (Ephesians 2:8-9) _____ Explain. _____

8. Can people earn their way to Heaven by giving generously to their church and to the needy? _____ Why? _____
_____

9. Can you become a Christian by being a faithful church member? _____
   Why? _____

10. Is a person saved by being baptized in water? _____ Why? _____
    _____

11. Is everyone who professes to be a Christian truly saved? _____ Why?
    _____

12. Is your own personal faith adequate to save you? _____ Why? (Galatians
    2:16; Romans 10:17; Ephesians 2:8-9) _____
    _____

13. Is it true that all religions lead us to God? _____ Why? (John 14:6) _____
    _____
    _____

14. Is it sufficient to be sincere in your religion in order to achieve salvation?
    _____ Why? _____

15. Was Saul well-educated and prepared in his religion? _____ How do you know?
    (Acts 22:1-3) _____

16. Did Saul love and help the Christians before his conversion to Jesus Christ?
    _____ How do you know? (Acts 22:4; Galatians 1:13) _____
    _____

17. Did Saul believe in God before his conversion to Jesus Christ? _____
    How do you know? (Acts 22:3) _____

18. Could Saul's fervent belief in God before his conversion have saved him
    from eternal condemnation? _____ Why? _____
    _____

19. Saul saw a bright light and heard the voice of Jesus Christ. Did that
    experience save him? _____ How do you know? _____
    _____

20. If you have an extraordinary religious experience, is that proof that you are
    saved? _____ How do you know? _____
    _____

21. Was Saul's life transformed by being baptized? _____ What does the word "baptism" mean? _____

22. Saul repented of his sin, trusted Jesus Christ as his Savior and give himself to Jesus Christ. Was Saul saved from eternal condemnation as a result of his conversion? _____ How do you know? (Romans 8:1; 2nd Timothy 1:12)
_____
_____

23. If you believe that Jesus Christ is God, does that belief save you? _____ Why? (James 2:18-19)_____
_____

24. Just because there has been a change or reformation in an individual's life, does this prove that he is a true Christian? _____ Why? _____
_____

25. If Jesus Christ has transformed the life of a person, is that proof of a true conversion? _____ Why? _____
_____

26. Please memorize 2nd Corinthians 5:17 and express it in your own words.
_____
_____
_____
_____

Do you feel that your personal life is pleasing to God? _____

Do you recognize that your life is not in harmony with God? _____

Note: If you do not have a person to help you study these lessons, please send your answers to the review questions or any doubts that you might have regarding this lesson to the Bible Institute Correspondence Department: philippi@becoming-a-christian.org

Becoming a Christian Organization, Inc.
6465 99th Way N. #17 B
St. Petersburg, FL 33708
727-393-7846

Chapter Two

The Universal Problem: Sin

For all have sinned, and come short of the Glory of God.

Romans 3:23

IN THE BEGINNING EVERYTHING WAS CREATED BY GOD IN TOTAL PERFECTION.

The Word of God speaks little about *eternity past*. We do know that God is eternal, and in "eternity past" He created the angels first. Later, God created the world, everything visible and invisible, in total perfection in six days (Genesis 1-2). Even though there is no proof that supports their theories, many deny or ignore the fact that the universe, and everything in it, was created by Almighty God. Although many do not believe God's Word, they are responsible to give an account of their deeds before God on Judgment Day. God warns us in Hebrews 9:27, *And as it is appointed unto men once to die, but after this the _____.* With this declaration, it is fitting to say that the God of the Bible is completely in charge. All human theories, including evolution, are tremendous lies that have their origin in Satan. They deny God's existence, His works and His purposes for all mankind.

Job, who was a true follower of God, desired to argue with God showing his own wisdom. God responded, in Job 38:1-7, with many questions about the creation of the world and even asked him about eternity past: *Who is this that darkeneth counsel by words without knowledge? Gird up now thy loins like a man; for I will demand of thee, and answer thou me. Where*

13

wast thou when I laid the _____ *of the earth? Declare, if thou hast understanding. Who hath laid the measures thereof, if thou knowest? Or who hath stretched the line upon it? Whereupon are the foundations thereof fastened? Or who laid the corner stone thereof; when the morning stars sang together, and all the sons of God* [the angels] *shouted for joy?* God witnessed everything that happened, for He created it all.

I. WHEN DID THE FIRST SIN OCCUR?

Ezekiel 28:11-19 explains how the angel Lucifer sinned against God. In verse 17 it says: *Thine* _____ *was lifted up because of thy beauty, thou hast corrupted thy wisdom by reason of thy brightness: I will cast thee to the ground, I will lay thee before kings, that they may behold thee.* Sin did not exist before Lucifer sinned and became Satan. Because of his vanity, pride, greed and jealousy, the angel Lucifer rebelled against God, thereby committing the first sin. The sin of Lucifer took place when he placed his own will above the will of God, desiring to be equal to God.

II. HOW DID SIN ENTER INTO THE WORLD?

In Genesis 2:16-17, God gave instructions to Adam as to what he could and could not eat: *And the Lord God commanded the man, saying, Of every tree of the garden thou mayest freely eat: But of the* _____ *of the knowledge of good and evil, thou shalt not eat of it:* **for in the day that thou eatest thereof thou shalt surely die.** Eating from the tree, after it had been forbidden by God, gave man the knowledge of evil. *Evil* can be defined as "disobedience to God." Man already had the knowledge of "good" from the first day of his creation.

Sin entered into the human race by means of deception and disobedience, motivated by disbelief. Eve listened to the voice of Satan, was tempted, fell into his trap of deceit and ate of the prohibited fruit. Adam knew that his wife had disobeyed God, but he did not want to abandon her; therefore, he ate of the fruit. He understood completely what he was doing, yet sinned, participating in that which God had prohibited. The Apostle Paul carefully explained this in 1st Timothy 2:14: *Adam was* _____ *deceived, but the woman being deceived was in the transgression.*

Every human being is comprised of a body, soul and spirit. When Adam and Eve sinned what part of them immediately died? Man's body is world-conscious, man's soul is self-conscious and man's spirit is God-conscious. Because they had sinned their spirit died, as God had warned them. It is obvious that their body didn't immediately die, nor their soul; however, their disobedience brought an immediate separation between them and God.

1. Did Adam and Eve understand that they had disobeyed God? (Genesis 3:6-7) _____

2. What part of Adam and Eve immediately died when they sinned? _____

3. Did they realize that they had lost the glory of God, which had clothed them? _____

4. What did they do to try to hide their nakedness? _____ _____

5. Were Adam and Eve sincere by trying to cover up their nakedness and the evidence of their sin? _____

6. Were their efforts sufficient to cover the evidence of their sinful condition? _____

Adam and Eve did something terrible by disobeying God. Their personal efforts were not sufficient to cover or correct the wrong they had done. With all this they could not get rid of their sin; they could only cover some of the visible evidence with fig leaves, which was accusing their conscience. It was not possible through their efforts to have fellowship restored with God, nor could it bring contentment and peace to their hearts. Both Adam and Eve were sincere, but their sincerity was not sufficient to correct their sinful condition. Why? _____ _____

We read in Genesis 3:8-10 that God went to the Garden of Eden to visit Adam and Eve. When they heard His voice they were ashamed. What did they try to do? _____ They had done their very best, but their best was not sufficient to hide the evidence of their sin. They had failed, but God's perfect provision is revealed in the brief account in Genesis 3:21: *Unto Adam also and to his wife did the LORD God make coats of* _____, *and clothed them.* As proof of His forgiveness God sacrificed animals, shedding their blood in order to cover the sin of Adam and Eve. God made coats of skins from the animals that were sacrificed to cover Adam and Eve's nakedness. Before they were expelled from the Garden of Eden, God gave the promise that the *Lamb of God* would come to this world to be sacrificed, shedding His blood to pay for all of our sin. This promise, given in Genesis 3:15, predicts the great victory that the Seed of Adam, the Lord Jesus Christ, would have over Satan. Jesus Christ would die on the cross for our sin and be raised again from the dead for our salvation.

In Romans 5:12 the Apostle Paul explained why we are all sinners: *Wherefore, as by one man sin entered into the world, and death by sin; and so death _____ upon all men, for that all have sinned.* We must understand that sin not only had its roots in Adam and Eve, but also is passed on to us at conception and has corrupted our lives since birth. Sin always turns us away from God. All human beings are sinners because of the original sin of disobedience. This sinful nature continues to be passed on from a father to his children and thus sin is passed on to everyone who comes into this world. Why do we sin? The reason we sin is because we are sinners. Never can we become sinners because we commit our first sin! **We sin because we are sinners**. It is very important that we have this clear. Never can a religious ritual remove or pardon our *original sin*. We are sinners and for this reason we sin.

III. WHAT IS SIN?

Sin is the act that violates all moral and divine laws that are portrayed in the Bible, among which are the Ten Commandments given in Exodus 20:3-17. Fundamentally, sin is rebellion against or resistance to the direction of all supreme authority. It is also enmity toward, avoidance of, or hatred of what God declares "good."

1. **"Missing the mark" is sin**. In the ancient Greek (the original language of the New Testament), *sin* means – "missing the bulls-eye on the target." We can strive to do the best we can (there is nothing wrong with that), but no one can reach the mark of perfection and holiness that God requires to enable us to enter heaven. All human beings are guilty of having sinned. Romans 3:10 affirms, *There are _____ righteous, no, not one.* Romans 3:23 says, *For _____ have sinned, and come short of the glory of God.* We **all** miss the mark!

2. **The infraction or transgression of God's Law is sin**. God declares in 1st John 3:4 that *whosoever committeth sin transgresseth also the*

16

_____: *for sin is the transgression of the Law.* Every transgression of the Law of God is sin. There may be exceptions to human laws, but no one can be exempt from God's Laws.

3. **All injustice is sin**. Proverbs 17:15 declares, *He that justifieth the wicked, and he that condemneth the _____, even they both are abomination* [great hatred] *to the Lord.* The word, *just* signifies – "right or correct." The word, *injustice* is "unfairness or wrongness." 1st John 5:17 declares that *All unrighteousness is sin.*

4. **Deceitfulness is sin**. When the truth is twisted, it is sin. The Apostle Paul warns in Romans 1:18, *The _____ of God is revealed from Heaven against all ungodliness and unrighteousness of men, who hold* [hold back] *the truth in unrighteousness.* To hold back the truth refers to twisting the truth. 2nd Peter 3:16 teaches us that men who are *unlearned and unstable wrest* [distort] *the Word of God.* This is illustrated in Isaiah 5:20: *Woe unto them that call _____ good, and _____ evil; that put darkness for light, and light for darkness; that put bitter for sweet, and sweet for bitter!* The word, *woe* in this case signifies – "the judgment or condemnation of God."

5. **Rebellion against God is sin**. Rebellion against God and His Word brings terrible consequences. God declares in 1st Samuel 15:23, *For rebellion is as the sin of witchcraft, and stubbornness is as iniquity and idolatry.* We should not take this sin lightly for God considers rebellion to be a terrible offense against Him. Joshua 1:18 gives the warning, *Whosoever he be that doth _____ against thy commandment, and will not hearken unto thy words in all that thou commandest him, he shall be put to death: only be strong and of a good courage.* Pride and arrogance have been found in the heart of man ever since Satan tempted Eve in the Garden of Eden, and it reveals itself in the form of rebellion. Proverbs 8:13 states, *The fear of the Lord is to hate _____: pride, and arrogancy, and the evil way, and the froward mouth, do I hate.* God requires obedience and hates rebellion.

6. **Disobedience is sin**. The sin of disobedience is related to the sin of rebellion. Disobeying God is to rebel against Him. 1st Timothy 1:9-10 teaches, *Knowing this, that the law is not made for a righteous man, but for the lawless and _____ for the ungodly and for sinners, for unholy and profane, for murderers of fathers and*

murderers of mothers, for manslayers, for whoremongers, for them that defile themselves with mankind, for menstealers, for liars, for perjured persons, and if there be any other thing that is contrary to sound doctrine. God's Word declares that they love their sins and their lives are out of control. Practicing sin is a **deliberate decision**. Ephesians 2:1-2 shows what a person was before giving himself to the Lord Jesus Christ: *Wherein in time past ye walked according to the course of this world, according to the prince of the power of the air, the spirit that now worketh in the children of* _____. If we are disobedient to what God requires, it is sin.

7. **Unbelief is sin.** 1st John 5:10 says, *He that believeth* [deposits all his confidence] *on the Son of God hath the witness in himself: he that* _____ *not God, hath made him a liar; because he believeth not the record that God gave of His Son.* If we do not wholly trust in what God has declared, we are saying that God is a liar. What does the Bible say regarding the end of those who do not believe Him? The answer is found in Revelation 21:8: *But the fearful, and* _____, *and abominable, and murderers, and whore-mongers, and sorcerers, and idolaters, and all liars, shall have their part in the lake which burneth with fire and brimstone: which is the second death.*

8. **Ungodliness is sin.** A godly life is a life faithful to God in all thoughts, attitudes, actions, worship and devotion. The word, *ungodliness* is the exact opposite of God's holiness. Jude 1:15 declares that the Lord is coming *to execute judgment upon all, and to convince all that are ungodly among them of all their* _____ *deeds which they have ungodly committed, and of all their hard speeches which **ungodly sinners** have spoken against him.* Proverbs 13:6 affirms, *Righteousness keepeth him that is upright in the way: but wickedness overthroweth the sinner.*

9. **All iniquity is sin.** *Iniquity* is any action against the character of God and against the moral order that God has given to mankind. As darkness is the absence of light, so is iniquity the absence of the perfect justice of God. Galatians 5:19-21 mentions some of the iniquities that God hates: *Now the **works of the** _____ are manifest, which are these; Adultery, fornication, uncleanness* [moral distortions], *lasciviousness* [lust or lewdness], *idolatry, witchcraft, hatred, variance* [a desire to bypass regulations],

emulations [ambition to equal or surpass in an evil way], *wrath, strife, seditions* [discord], *heresies* [distortions of doctrinal truths], *envyings, murders, drunkenness, revellings* [wild celebrations or orgies], *and such like: of the which I tell you before, as I have also told you in time past, that they which do such things shall not inherit the kingdom of God.* People are involved in these types of iniquities (sins) because it is part of their sinful **fleshly** nature.

10. **All lying is sin.** Is a "white lie" a sin, or just a convenience? There is no such thing as a white lie. All lies will eventually cause harm and are terrible in the sight of God. In John 8:44, Jesus Christ tells where all lies come from. Where do lies come from? _____
    1st Timothy 4:1-2 teaches us that some will depart from the faith, *speaking _____ in hypocrisy; having their **conscience seared** with a hot iron.* To live a lie is actually hypocrisy. Many people lie without remorse, because it is part of their nature. Proverbs 6:16-19 speaks of the hatred that God has for the sin of untruthfulness. God requires a life of honesty.

11. **Stealing is sin.** Among the Ten Commandments in Exodus 20:15, God commands, *Thou shalt not _____.* There are many ways that you can be guilty of stealing. For example, taking something that does not belong to you, even small items, is stealing. Also, it is stealing when you borrow something and do not return it. To destroy someone's reputation is stealing, and perhaps impossible to remedy. The Apostle Paul warns us in Ephesians 4:28, *Let him that stole _____ no more: but rather let him labor, working with his hands the thing which is good, that he may have to give to him that needeth.* Many thieves escape man's attention, but God sees them, and they can never escape God's judgment.

12. **All filthy and corrupt talk is sin.** In Ephesians 4:29, God orders us to *let no _____ communication proceed out of your mouth, but that which is good to the use of edifying, that it may minister grace unto the hearers.* There are many ways that a corrupt mouth manifests sin. You can recognize it by the colored jokes, the cursing, the perverse conversations, the gossip, the slander, the crude talk, the ridicule, etc. The Lord Jesus Christ declared in Luke 6:45, *A good man out of the good treasure of his heart bringeth forth that which is _____; and an evil man out of the evil treasure of his heart*

bringeth forth that which is _____ *: for of the abundance of the heart his mouth speaketh.* Proverbs 4:24 orders, *Put away from thee a froward* [uncontrolled] *mouth, and perverse lips put far from thee.* We are all responsible before God for each word that leaves our lips. King Solomon declared in Proverbs 10:19, *In the multitude of words there wanteth* [lacks] *not sin: but he that* _____ *his lips is wise.*

13. **The failure to fulfill our responsibilities and obligations is sin.** This sin of omission is committed when we do not fulfill our physical and spiritual responsibilities, at home, at church, at work, etc. James 4:17 says, *Therefore to him that knoweth to do* _____, *and doeth it not, to him it is sin.* God makes us responsible for the "good" that **we do not do!** Many are not interested in reading the Bible or understanding God's will for their lives. This indifference toward God and His Word is sin.

14. **The unwillingness to forgive is sin.** In Matthew 6:12-15, Jesus Christ instructs His followers to ask for forgiveness and also forgive: *And* _____ *us our debts,* [sins] *as we forgive our debtors* [those that have sinned against us]. *And lead us not into temptation, but deliver us from evil: For thine is the kingdom, and the power, and the glory, forever. Amen. For if ye forgive men their trespasses* [offences], *your Heavenly Father will also forgive you: But if ye forgive not men their trespasses* [offences], *neither will your Father forgive your trespasses* [offences]. Jesus Christ warns, if you refuse to forgive someone for the evil that they have committed against you, He will not forgive you. Hebrews 12:15 cautions us of the damaging results of not forgiving, because bitterness will grow in your heart to the extent that it will destroy you and will affect others.

15. **The sin that condemns everyone to Hell is that of not believing (to not deposit full confidence) in Jesus Christ as their Savior** as it says in John 3:18: *He that believeth on him is not condemned: but he that believeth not is condemned already, because he hath* _____ *believed in the name of the only begotten Son of God.* John 16:8-9 mentions three principle works of the Holy Spirit: *And when he is come, he will reprove the world of* _____, *and of righteousness, and of judgment: Of* _____, *because they believe not on me.* Notice it does not say, convicts the world of **sins.** A person is not really convicted of the seriousness of his sin if we only

talk about whether he lies, cheats, is unfair or commits adultery, etc. **We obviously understand that God condemns all of these sins; however, the conviction, which the Bible is talking about here, is the sin of not believing on Jesus Christ.** God uses this issue of unbelief to confront everyone. We have no reason to expect anything from God if we live in rejection of Jesus Christ. Frankly, we all have rebelled against God! We need to be convicted of our rejection of the authority of Jesus Christ over our life. In Acts 5:29-33, the Apostle Peter proclaimed in his message to Israel, "You killed the Lord Jesus Christ, but God raised Him from the dead." **The fact is that we all were in opposition to God until we surrendered ourselves to Him.**

IV. WE ALL ARE SINNERS.

The Pharisees were the most important religious leaders in Israel. Besides interpreting and teaching the Law of the Old Testament, they taught their own religious laws. They pretended to be very spiritual, but Jesus Christ revealed their true identity in Luke 18:9-12. The Jews had been enslaved to the oppression of the legalism of the Pharisees. *Legalism* is any human effort that seeks to make a person holy by following laws. In John 8:3-11 Jesus Christ identified them as sinners and utterly devoid of personal righteousness. No matter which religion is represented in the world, all their leaders are sinners as affirmed in Romans 3:23: *For all have sinned, and come short of the glory of God.*

Please answer the following questions to the best of your ability:

1. Although the Pharisees considered themselves to be very religious, according to Luke 18:9-12, with whom was he praying? _____ According to Psalm 66:18, was this Pharisee's prayer heard by God? _____

2. Was the righteousness (religiosity and good works) of the Pharisees sufficient to gain them entrance into Heaven? _____ Why? (Matthew 5:20) _____

    _____

3. What concept did the Pharisees have of themselves? _____

4. Are all religious leaders sinners? _____ Why? (Romans 3:23) _____

    _____

    Could there be any exceptions? _____

The publicans were despised because they were dishonest tax collectors. They were Jews working directly in allegiance with the Roman government. They also embezzled money from their own people. They were hated and considered to be terrible sinners. In Luke 18:13-14 Jesus Christ identified them as sinners.

Please answer the following questions to the best of your ability:

1. Why were the tax collectors so despised? _____
    _____

2. In what condition did the publican find himself before God? _____
    _____
    _____

3. In Luke 5:27-32 we have an account about another publican. Who was Levi? _____

4. What was Levi doing when Jesus called him? _____
    _____

5. Why did the Pharisees think it was terrible that Jesus ate with the publicans? _____
    _____

6. What concept did the Pharisees have of the publicans?_____
    _____

7. In the illustration in Luke 5:31-32, what do the following represent?

    • "The sick" represent the _____.

    • "The doctor" represents _____.

    • Those who feel "healthy" represent those who believe themselves to be _____.

8. Can a doctor do anything for a person who does not consider himself to be sick? _____ Why? _____
    _____

9. Why did Jesus Christ come to this world, according to Luke 5:32?
    _____
    _____

10. There are many that minimize the seriousness of their sin. Is God able to save those who do not recognize that they are terrible sinners? _____Why? _____

_____

11. Can Jesus Christ save a sinner who has not truly repented of his sin? _____ Why? (Luke 5:32) _____

12. Are more "bad" people or more "good" people converted to Christ? _____ Why? _____

_____

13. Luke 19:1-10 tells about another publican who was converted to Christ. Who put into the heart of Zacchaeus the curiosity and desire to see Jesus? _____

14. What two evidences in the life of Zacchaeus show that he was truly transformed by Jesus Christ? (1) _____

_____

(2) _____

_____

15. Who are you really deceiving if you think you can hide the sin that you commit? Others?_____ God? _____ Yourself? _____

V. THERE IS NONE RIGHTEOUS BEFORE GOD.

In the book of Mark we see the tragedy of a selfish, self-righteous, superficial seeker who approached Jesus with an important question. Note how Jesus answered his need in Mark 10:17-22, *And when he was gone forth into the way, there came one running, and kneeled to him, and asked him, Good Master* [or teacher], *what shall I do that I may inherit eternal life? And Jesus said unto him, Why callest thou me good? There is none good but one, that is, God.* This young ruler of a synagogue ran up to Him, kneeling down said, "Good Master... good teacher." He not only acknowledged Jesus as a legitimate teacher, but as a good person. Where is the problem? Amazingly, it comes up where you wouldn't expect it. The problem is revealed in one word in verse 17, it is the word "**good**." If there is any word that most people do not understand, it is the word, "good." Ask anybody, "Are you a good person?" What are they going to say? "Of course, I'm a good person."

It is a term loosely used, because we believe ourselves to be good. This young man considered himself to be good, for he taught the things of God; therefore, he associated Jesus with himself as being "good." How did Jesus answer him? No words of faith ever mentioned. No comment about believing is ever stated, because the issue here is **this young man's sin, the supreme Law of God and the lack of repentance.**

Our Lord makes this clear in one profound statement. *Why callest thou me good?* ***There is none good but one, that is, God.*** Does that change your definition of good? Does that have some effect on it? No one is good except God alone. That makes "good" completely absolute, not relative. There are relative degrees of "bad." Many feel that they are not as bad as someone else, but none of us is good. Only God is good! That is a smashing blow for a legalist.

Before we can talk about the gospel, before we can talk about salvation, before we can talk about eternal life and the workings of God, we must understand that we are not good. That man had no true idea of goodness; therefore, he had no real understanding of the Law of God which he carelessly studied or he would not have casually used the word "good" and labeled a stranger with it. The Law is holy, just and good. True goodness is the nature of God and the true goodness of the nature of God is revealed in the Word of God. When we measure ourselves against the Law of God, we are not a good. We are "bad." We are terrible sinner!

The purpose of the Law is to show how perfectly good God is and how utterly evil man is, thus producing guilt, fear, dread and remorse for our sin. This is the first step toward becoming a true Christian.

Read Romans 3:9-10.

1. In the sight of God, who is better, the religious Jew or the pagan Gentile? _____

    _____

2. Are we better than the Jews? _____

3. How many "just" or "good" people are there according to the Word of God? _____

Read Romans 3:23 and Romans 5:12.

4. How many people have sinned? _____ We know that Jesus Christ is God and could not have sinned. Is it possible that there has been another person that has lived on this earth who has not sinned? _____ If so, who? _____

5. When sin entered into the world through Adam and Eve, what punishment did they receive as a result of their sin? (Genesis 2:17; Romans 5:12) _____ Was it spiritual death or physical death or both?
   _____

6. According to Genesis 5:5, to what type of death does this refer?
   _____

7. Does Ephesians 2:1 speak of physical death or spiritual death? _____
   _____

8. Is there something that man can do **by his own power** to change his sinful condition in order to please God? _____ If so, what? _____
   _____

9. According to Isaiah 64:6, how does God see our righteousness? *But we are all as an unclean thing, and all our righteousnesses are as filthy rags; and we all do fade as a leaf; and our iniquities, like the wind, have taken us away.* _____

10. According to Matthew 5:27-28, **underline the correct answer:**

    a. (True) or (False) Whether by act or thought, without exception, everyone is a sinner.

    b. (True) or (False) If you are sincere and not doing harm to others, it is really not important what you do or think.

    c. (True) or (False) We can disobey the commandments of God with our thoughts as well as our actions.

VI. THE CONSEQUENCES OF SIN

1. Sin brings terrible consequences to our life. After the first sin was committed by Adam and Eve, which is explained in Genesis 3:1-24, God pronounced judgment upon the serpent, upon Satan, upon Eve

and upon Adam. Their sinful nature was then passed on to all their descendents. They never thought that the consequences of their sin would be so severe. Sin will always bring consequences far beyond what we had ever imagined. Sickness, pain, physical and eternal death are the results of sin. Ever since then, the whole world has been affected by their sin.

It is necessary for God to judge and punish the sins of each person individually. We have all been condemned to eternal punishment. We understand the seriousness of sin when we contemplate the great judgment of God that the Son of God had to suffer for our sins on the cross. That judgment, which was focused directly upon Jesus Christ by God the Father, was so terrible that He could not look upon Him. Matthew 27:46 expresses his anguish: *Jesus cried with a loud voice, saying, Eli, Eli, lama sabachthani? That is to say, My God, my God, why hast thou _____ me?* We are not told how God poured out his wrath upon Jesus Christ, but it was greater than all the punishment that man could have ever invented. Jesus Christ, as our substitute, suffered this terrible punishment for our sins.

2. Sin causes division between God and us. Sin causes us to continue in our sin much longer than we had planned. The prophet Isaiah declared in Isaiah 59:2, *But your iniquities* (sins) *have separated between you and your God, and your _____ have hid his face from you, that he will not hear.* God, in His perfection and holiness, cannot have fellowship with sinful man, the crown of His creation, while there exists a barrier of sin between man and Himself. This is explained in Habakkuk 1:13: *Thou art of purer eyes than to behold evil, and canst not _____ on iniquity.* There would be a great separation between God and mankind if it were not for the love and work of the Lord Jesus Christ when He died on the cross for us. This is affirmed in 1st Timothy 2:5-6: *For there is one God, and one mediator between God and men, the man Christ Jesus; Who gave himself a ransom for all, to be testified in due time.*

3. Sin deceives us. Psalm 7:14 presents the process of deceit: *Behold, he travaileth with iniquity, and hath conceived mischief, and brought forth falsehood.* At first sin presents itself in a different way from what it really is. Those who believe that they can play with the fire of sin without getting burned are living in great deception. In 2nd

Timothy 3:13 the Apostle Paul warns us about what will happen: *But evil men and seducers shall wax worse and worse, _____, and being deceived.* We are warned in 1st John 1:8 not to deceive ourselves: *If we say that we have no sin, we deceive ourselves, and the truth is not in us.* **Sin takes us beyond where we planned to go!**

4. Sin can cause sickness. The Apostle Paul cautioned the church in 1st Corinthians 11:28-30: *But let a man examine* [judge sin in his life] *himself, and so let him eat of that bread, and drink of that cup. For he that eateth and drinketh unworthily, eateth and drinketh damnation to himself, not discerning the Lord's body. For this cause many are weak and* _____ *among you, and many sleep* (died).

5. Sin robs us of the joy that only God can give. King David expressed his profound repentance toward God in Psalm 51:8-12: *Make me to hear joy and gladness; that the bones which thou hast broken may rejoice. Hide thy face from my sins, and blot out all mine iniquities. Create in me a clean heart, O God; and renew a right spirit within me. Cast me not away from thy presence; and take not thy Holy Spirit from me. Restore unto me the* _____ *of thy salvation; and uphold me with thy free spirit.*

6. Sin brings death, physical and spiritual death, and after that the judgment of God. Romans 6:23 clearly states, *For the wages of sin is death.* God declared in Ezekiel 18:4, *the soul that sinneth, it shall* _____. Hebrews 9:27 confirms that they will be judged: *And as it is appointed unto men once to die, but after this the* _____. The Apostle Paul declared in Acts 17:31, *He* [God] *hath appointed a day, in the which **He will judge the world in righteousness** by that man* [Jesus Christ] *whom he hath ordained.*

7. Sin brings the punishment of eternal condemnation. This condemnation separates every lost sinner from God and brings the punishment upon every lost sinner for all eternity. Revelation 21:8 mentions some of those who will be there: *But the fearful, and unbelieving, and abominable, and murderers, and whoremongers, and sorcerers, and idolaters, and all liars, shall have their part in the lake which burneth with* _____ *and brimstone: which is the second death.* This punishment is terrible and beyond our comprehension. Revelation 20:11-15 reveals how this judgment

takes place: *And I saw a great white throne, and him that sat on it, from whose face the earth and the Heaven fled away; and there was found no place for them. And I saw the dead, small and great, stand before God; and the books were opened: and another book was opened, which is the book of life: and the dead were _____ out of those things which were written in the books, according to their works. And the sea gave up the dead, which were in it; and death and Hell delivered up the dead which were in them: and they were judged every man according to their works. And death and Hell were cast into the _____ of fire. This is the second _____.* This death is not annihilation, but the condition of all the resurrected unsaved to receive their deserved and just punishment for all eternity, first in Hell and later in the Lake of Fire: *And whosoever was not found written in the book of life was cast into the Lake of Fire.* The true Christian will not be in this judgment, for he will be with Jesus Christ in Heaven, because his name is written in the *Book of Life*. **Sin cost a lot more than you could ever pay!**

VII. MAN TRIES TO JUSTIFY HIMSELF IN VAIN.

1. A human tendency is to justify one's self. In Luke 16:15 Jesus Christ accused the Pharisees saying, *Ye are they which _____ yourselves before men; but God knoweth your hearts: for that which is highly esteemed among men is abomination in the sight of God.*

2. Many consider themselves to be very wise. The prophet pronounced judgment on them in Isaiah 5:21: *Woe* [condemnation] *unto them that are wise in their own eyes, and prudent in their own sight!* Proverbs 14:12 declared, *There is a way which seemeth _____ unto a man, but the end thereof are the ways of death.* There are those who are convinced that God doesn't exist, and proudly make fun of the Bible, scoffing at the coming judgment of God. At the moment they die they will realize the truth, but too late.

3. Many deny the fact that someday they will have to give an account of themselves to God. In Hebrews 4:12-13 God affirms, *For the word of God is quick, and powerful, and sharper than any twoedged sword, piercing even to the dividing asunder of soul and spirit, and of the joints and marrow, and is a discerner of the thoughts and intents of the heart. Neither is there any creature that is not manifest in his sight: but all things are naked and opened unto the _____*

of him with whom we have to do [give an account]. Also, Numbers 32:23 says, *be sure your sins will find you out.* Our tendency is to try to convince ourselves that we are not all that bad. Galatians 6:7 declares, *Be not deceived; God is not mocked: for whatsoever a man soweth, that shall he also reap.* God cannot accept excuses for our sin. Can we possibly deceive God? _____

4. There are those who desire to hide their activities from God, thinking that He doesn't pay attention to details. In Luke 12:1-3 we read, *In the mean time, when there were gathered together an innumerable multitude of people, insomuch that they trode one upon another, he began to say unto his disciples first of all, Beware ye of the leaven of the Pharisees, which is hypocrisy. For there is _____ covered, that shall not be revealed; neither _____, that shall not be known. Therefore, whatsoever ye have spoken in darkness shall be heard in the light; and that which ye have spoken in the ear in closets shall be proclaimed upon the housetops.* What did Jesus refer to when he warned them about the "hypocrisy of the Pharisees?" He warned them against the sin of deception, pride and arrogance. Aren't we all guilty in one way or another of hypocrisy? _____ Most of the time we are more concerned about what people think of us and little about what God sees in us. Why? _____

Realizing this problem, we should pay attention to Jeremiah 16:17: *For mine eyes are upon all their ways: they are not _____ from my face, neither is their iniquity* (sin) *hid from mine eyes.* Jeremiah 23:24 asks, *Can any hide himself in secret places that I shall not _____ him? saith the Lord. Do not I fill heaven and earth? saith the Lord.* Will those things that we thought were secrets be revealed some day? _____ In view of the fact that it is impossible to hide anything from God, we should not try to ignore or forget the problem of sins in our life? Mark 4:22 affirms, *For there is nothing hid, which shall not be manifested; neither was any thing kept _____, but that it should come abroad.* God confirms in Ecclesiastes 12:14 the reality of the coming judgment: *For God shall bring every work into judgment, with every secret thing, whether it be _____ or whether it be _____.* Knowing that we are responsible to God for what we do and what we are, what should be our response? _____

VIII. HOW DO YOU SEE YOUR OWN CONDITION?

Read Romans 6:16 and John 8:34.

1. In some way are you trying to avoid the scrutiny of those who know you? _____ Why? _____

2. How do you see your condition before God? _____
   Please explain. _____
   _____

3. Are you satisfied with the direction that your life is presently going, or do you want to change? _____

In light of what we have read in God's Word, what type of a sinner do you consider yourself? Please examine your own heart and life and put an "X" on the line that best illustrates your sinful condition.

(a) Little _____ (b) Better than most _____ (c) Average _____
(d) Very great sinner _____ or (e) Terrible sinner _____.

According to God's Word what kind of a sinner are you in the sight of God? _____

SUMMARY:

Although many do not believe the Word of God, they will still have to give account of themselves before God in the Day of Judgment. Why do we sin? We have to understand that sin has its roots in Adam and Eve, but it also enters into every human being at the time of conception. Sin always separates us from God. All human beings are sinful because of the original sin of disobedience. This sinful nature continues to pass from parents to children. The reason we sin is because we are sinners. In no way do we become sinners when we commit our first sin! **We sin because we are sinners!** It is important that we understand this truth. There are no religious rituals or rites that can remove or forgive the original sin that is found in everyone. "Sin takes you beyond where you planned to go, it makes you stay there longer than you planned to stay, and you will find that it costs a lot more than you could ever pay!"

1st Timothy 1:15 tell us *that Christ Jesus came into the world to save sinners.* For who did Christ Jesus die? _____ Romans 5:6 says, *For when we were yet without strength, in due time Christ died for the ungodly.* Romans5:8

confirms, *But God commendeth his love toward us, in that, while we were yet sinners, Christ died for us.* Christ died for you. Jesus Christ declared in John 3:16, *For God so loved the world, that he gave his only begotten Son, that whosoever believeth* [trust completely] *in him should not perish, but have everlasting life.* Luke 5:32 declares the great truth that Jesus Christ cannot do anything for those who do not consider themselves to be terrible sinners. Jesus did not come to make bad people good, but to give **dead** people, true **life**. Many have a fatalistic attitude about the future saying, "what will be, will be." It doesn't have to be this way. God wants you to repent of your sins and surrender yourself to Him with all your heart.

REVIEW QUESTIONS - CHAPTER 2

THE UNIVERSAL PROBLEM: SIN

1. What is the universal problem? _____

2. Everyone in the world is a sinner; however, we know that Jesus Christ was not a sinner. Is it possible that there was another person who lived on this earth, who was not a sinner ? _____

3. Why is it necessary for God to judge and punish everyone's sin? (Romans 3:19) _____

4. Is the first step toward salvation your recognition of the fact that you are a terrible sinner? _____ Why? _____
    _____

5. In order for God to save you, is it necessary to repent of your sins? _____

6. If man tries as hard as he can, and lives the best he can, is he able to gain entrance into Heaven by his good works? _____ Why? _____
    _____

7. Is it possible to help God save you by doing good deeds? _____

8. Is it true that those who have sinned much are further from salvation than those who have sinned little? _____ Why? (Romans 3:10, 23) _____
    _____

9. Does the true Christian always have to battle against sin? _____ Why? (Ephesians 6:11-17) _____
    _____

Underline the correct answer: (True) or (False).

10. (True) or (False) Your good works and good behavior can justify you in God's sight.

11. (True) or (False) Religious rites, rituals or good works cannot solve the problem of sin. The only solution for sin is through the redemption that Jesus Christ provided by dying on the cross and rising again from the dead.

12. (True) or (False) We can pay for our sins by doing certain penitence.

13. (True) or (False) In order to have the salvation that God has provided, first you have to recognize that you are a terrible sinner.

14. (True) or (False) We sin because we are sinners.

15. (True) or (False) We become sinners when we sin the first time.

16. (True) or (False) The Pharisees were humble religious leaders.

17. (True) or (False) Legalism or a strict obedience to God's Laws cannot produce a clean life, nor a pure heart.

18. (True) or (False) The publicans worked for the Roman government collecting taxes.

19. (True) or (False) We must confess our sins only to Jesus Christ and ask Him for forgiveness. (1st John 1:6-9)

20. (True) or (False) Jesus Christ is the only one who can forgive and cleanse you from all sins.

21. (True) or (False) Baptism can help cleanse you from all your sins.

22. Please memorize Romans 3:23 and express it in your own words. _____
   _____
   _____

Do you really recognize the condition of your heart? Study carefully the following chapter.

Chapter Three

Examining the Heart

The heart is deceitful above all things, and desperately wicked:
who can know it? I the LORD search the heart, I try the reins,
even to give every man according to his ways,
and according to the fruit of his doings.

Jeremiah 17:9-10

WHAT DOES THE BIBLE SAY ABOUT THE HEART?

The Bible speaks much about the heart of man and also the heart of God. What does 1ˢᵗ Samuel 16:7 teach regarding the heart? *The LORD seeth not as man seeth; for man looketh on the outward appearance, but the LORD looketh on the heart.* We form our opinions about people by their appearance and actions. How does God see that same person? _____

Read Mark 7:20-23 to comprehend the condition of the human heart. Jesus Christ said: *That which cometh out of the man, that defileth the man. For from within, out of the _____ of men, proceed evil thoughts, adulteries, fornications, murders, thefts, covetousness, wickedness, deceit, lasciviousness, an evil eye, blasphemy, pride, foolishness: All these evil things come from _____, and defile the man.* We must understand that the heart of all our problems is the condition of our heart!

I. THE BIBLICAL DEFINITION OF THE HEART

Proverbs 4:20-23 gives the admonition, *My son, attend to my words; incline thine ear unto my sayings. Let them not depart from thine eyes; keep them in the midst of thine _____. For they are life unto those that find them, and health to all their flesh. Keep thy heart with all diligence; for out of it are the issues of life.* Proverbs 28:25-26 declares, *He that is of a _____ heart stirreth up strife. . . He that trusteth in his own heart is a fool.*

What does the word, "heart" refer to in the previous verses? ***Underline the right answer.***

1. It is the organ that pumps the blood through the body.

2. It is the real interior part of a person that cannot be seen, the soul.

3. It is the visible behavior of the person.

II. THE CONDITION OF THE HEART WITHOUT CHRIST JESUS

Read once again Jeremiah 17:9-10.

1. What words did Jeremiah use to describe the condition of the heart?
   _____

2. Who examines the condition of our heart? _____

3. Why is it necessary for God to examine our heart? _____
   _____

III. THE CONTAMINATION OF THE HEART

We read in Matthew 15:1-10 about the religious leaders who used the traditions of their religion to make exemptions to the Law of God. This passage has to do with the obligation that the children had to help support their parents in their old age. By performing a religious ceremony, the children schemed together with the priests to be exempt of their personal responsibility to support their parents in their old age. This was committing a terrible injustice and revealed the contamination of their hearts.

Jesus said in Matthew 15:8-9, *This people draweth nigh unto me with their mouth, and honoureth me with their lips; but their _____ is far from me. But in vain they do worship me, teaching for doctrines the commandments of men.* Many religious people put great value on the exterior, their practices and religious traditions, but give little importance to the Word of God and the condition of their own heart. On one occasion the religious leaders accused Jesus Christ and His disciples for not performing the ceremonial washing of the hands before they ate.

Read Matthew 15:11-20.

1. Is it possible to contaminate our soul before God if we eat food that is not clean? _____

2. Is it possible to contaminate man's soul with what goes out of the mouth?_____ Why? _____
_____

3. Where do the sins that we commit originate? _____

4. According to Matthew 15:19, name one sin that is **internal**. _____
_____

5. According to Matthew 15:19, name six sins that are **external**. They also originate in the heart, but are visible.

   a. _____   d. _____
   b. _____   e. _____
   c. _____   f. _____

6. Where do we find **the root of our wickedness**? Is it found in the interior (what we are) or in the exterior (what we do)?_____

IV. THE CURE FOR THE SINFUL HEART

Read Psalm 51:10. Underline the correct answers.

1. It is important to recognize that the origin of our actions is: (the heart), (the mind), (our parents) or (the Bible).

2. We need to let our actions and attitudes be exposed to the Light of God by: (the Holy Spirit), (the preaching of the Word of God), (reading the Bible) or (all of the above).

3. It is not sufficient to just recognize that there is wickedness in our heart. To remedy the sinful condition of the heart it is necessary to pay attention to: (society), (education), (religion) or (the Word of God).

4. According to Matthew 5:8, what is the prerequisite to see God? __

_____

Read Matthew 23:25-28 about the cleansing of the cup (our life), which illustrates the necessity of total cleansing.

5. What is the significance of the statement, *that which is **within** the cup and platter?* _____

6. What is the significance of the statement, *the **outside** of the cup and of the platter?* _____

V. THE RELATIONSHIP BETWEEN THE HEART AND ITS FRUITS

In Matthew 7:16-20, Christ uses the illustration of the tree and its fruit to show the relationship between our heart and our behavior. The tree has roots, trunk, branches, leaves and fruit. There are parts seen and parts not seen.

1. What part of the tree represents the conduct of man? _____

2. What part of the tree represents the heart? _____

3. What kind of fruit does a bad tree produce? _____
   What kind of fruit does a good tree produce? _____

4. What is the result of having an evil heart? _____

5. If you remove the bad fruit from a tree and hang good fruit on it, will it become a good tree? _____

6. Is it possible to grow oranges on apple trees? _____ Is it possible to produce spiritual fruit in a life which is contrary to God's nature? _____

7. If a person reforms his bad conduct by replacing it with good conduct, would that change the condition of his heart and make him a good person in the sight of God? _____

8. If a person receives a new heart from God, what changes will take place in his life? _____

_____

_____

VI. THE CLEANSING OF THE HEART IN VAIN

Many try to clean up their lives by means of religion, rites, rituals, good works or good conduct. Matthew 12:43-45 gives the example of a clean, but empty house: *When the unclean spirit is gone out of a man, he walketh through dry places, seeking rest, and findeth none. Then he saith, I will return into* **my house** *from whence I came out; and when he is come, he findeth it empty, swept, and garnished. Then goeth he, and taketh with himself _____ other spirits more _____ than himself, and they enter in and dwell there: and the last state of that man is worse than the first.*

1. After the wicked spirit had left the body and life of the individual, what was the condition of his life? _____ Did he have a permanent victory over that evil and wicked spirit? _____

2. When a person gets victory over a certain sin or sins in his life, but does not repent of his sin and give himself to Jesus Christ with all his heart, what can happen? _____

   _____

3. There are two words spoken by the evil spirit in verse 44, which show that the person did not belong to Jesus Christ. The unclean spirit said, *I will return into* _____ _____. The temporary change that was made could have been by the individual's efforts, or for the mere fact that the wicked spirit wanted to leave so that he could carry out his plan and create a situation worse than before.

4. Why did the house stay temporarily swept, garnished and adorned? _____What do the garnished things represent? _____

5. Does a reformation in the individual's life result in a complete transformation or something that is only temporary?_____ Why? _____

   _____

6. What were the final results of the return of the evil spirit to **his house**?

   _____

   _____

   _____

SUMMARY:

Have you taken time to examine your heart? The Apostle Paul, after confronting the church in Corinth regarding their worldly sinful ways, told them in 2nd Corinthians 13:5 to examine their heart and life to see if they were truly saved: *Examine yourselves, whether ye be in the* _____ [truly born-again]; ***prove your own selves***. *Know ye not your own selves, how that Jesus Christ is in you, except ye be reprobates?* God explains in Ezekiel 11:18-20 what He wants to do in your life: *And they shall come thither, and they shall take away all the detestable things thereof and all the abominations thereof from thence. And I will give them one* _____, *and I will put a new spirit within you; and I will take the stony heart out of their flesh, and will give them an* _____ *of flesh: That they may walk in my statutes, and keep mine ordinances, and do them: and they shall be* _____ *people, and I will be their God.* The only way that we can truly have a changed heart is by the work of God. Even though we always have to fight against sin in our new life as a true Christian, we receive the constant help of Jesus Christ who enables us to have the victory.

REVIEW QUESTIONS - CHAPTER 3

EXAMINING THE HEART

Answer <u>Yes</u> or <u>No</u>.

1. Sin was passed on to us at conception and has corrupted our lives since birth. _____

2. Is it possible to worship God with your mouth, but at the same time have your heart far from Him? (Matthew 15:8-9) _____

3. Is God aware of the condition of your heart? _____

4. Can a person always rely on the feelings that he has in his heart? _____ (Jeremiah 17:9)

5. If God has cleansed your heart and life, will your life reflect that cleansing? _____

6. Can religious practices, which are external, correct the evil that is in a person's heart? _____

7. Is it necessary to overcome your bad habits before God can cleanse your heart? _____

8. Will the things that come from your mouth show what is in your heart? (Matthew 15:18)_____

9. Can a person say good things about God, but at the same time have an evil heart? (Matthew 15:8)_____

10. Is it possible to change your bad behavior by your own willpower? _____

11. Will good behavior be permanent if it comes through reform? _____

12. Can God create in you a new heart and give you a new life? _____ Will it be permanent? _____

13. Please memorize Jeremiah 17:9-10 and express it in your own words.

    _____

    _____

    _____

    _____

    _____

Please continue studying the next lesson, which will help you understand who are the true sons of God.

Chapter Four

Who are the Sons of God?

He came unto his own, and his own received him not.
But as many as received him, to them gave he power to
become the sons of God, even to them that believe on His name.

John 1:11-12

Note: The phrase, "as many as received him," is the result of depositing your faith and confidence completely in the Lord Jesus Christ as your personal Savior.

NOT EVERYONE IS A SON OF GOD.

Many people have their own personal opinions as to the way to get to Heaven. Many insist that all human beings are sons of God because they have been born into a religious family, have been baptized or just because they are descendents of Adam. Even though all of these sources of authority occupy a predominate place in the lives of many, the true and only source of all authority for mankind is the written Word of God, the Holy Bible. Not everyone is a child of God! John 1:12 states clearly that we must *become the sons of God*.

I. THE AUTHORITY OF GOD'S WORD IS CONTRARY TO HUMAN PHILOSOPHIES.

1. Man's philosophies are full of errors.

There are many who believe that all religions will take you to the same God. This is not the truth! Those who make such a declaration have little concept of all the religions. Some beliefs do not admit the existence of a Superior Being. However, many insist that every human being is a "child of God," and that God will have compassion on them in the Final Judgment. They feel that God is so merciful and loving that He would not send them to eternal condemnation, for they do not consider themselves to be all that bad.

There are three different principle sources that many maintain as their religious authority. As a basis for knowing God, they rely on their **intelligence, their experiences or their traditions**. This is all that man can rely on when he does not have the truth of God's Word.

a. Their faith is based upon their **intellect**.

It is possible that a family member or a friend has planted doubts in your mind about God and His Word. They seek to promote intellectualism such as existentialism, metaphysics, mind control, scientology and cybernetics (Definitions on page 182), which are all philosophies of men. They are only nourishing their own egos. Some very sincere people say they are guided by their conscience. One should not ignore the fact that he might be very sincere, but at the same time be sincerely mistaken. The **intellect** and the conscience are not reliable guides, unless they are totally governed by the truth of the Word of God. The intellect is directed by what we learn and the conscience is directed by what we believe. The only reliable guide is the Word of God, the Bible. The Psalmist declared in Psalm 119:105, *Thy word is a lamp unto my feet, and a _____ unto my path.*

b. Their faith is based upon their **experiences**.

There are those who look for sensational experiences, such as special visions and revelations. They insist that these unusual experiences come from God. Their confidence is in themselves and their experiences, not in God's Word. They are also nourishing their own egos with deception!

The Apostles Peter, James and John had an unforgettable experience when they saw Jesus Christ transfigured. However, in 2nd Peter 1:16-21, the Apostle Peter declared, *For we have not followed cunningly devised fables, when we made known unto you the power and coming of our Lord Jesus Christ, but were eyewitnesses of his majesty. For he received from God the Father honor and glory, when there came such a voice to him from the excellent glory, This is my beloved Son, in whom I am well pleased. And this voice which came from Heaven we heard, when we were with him in the holy mount. We have also a more _____ word of prophecy; whereunto ye do well that ye take heed, as unto a light that shineth in a dark place, until the day dawn, and the day star arise in your hearts: Knowing this first, that no prophecy of the Scripture is of any private* [personal] *interpretation. For the prophecy came not in old time by the will of man: but holy men of God spake as they were moved* [inspired] *by the Holy Ghost.* The Apostle Peter teaches us that we can only accept what the Word of God says, and not base our faith on the experiences of men.

c. Their faith is based upon the **traditions of their religion**.

Many put their faith in the traditions of a church and try to stand firm on what their religion teaches. It is an act of depositing a **blind faith** in their religion, in their beliefs, in the sacraments, and certain rites or rituals, trying to earn their salvation. They are taught that it is a sin to doubt or to challenge any belief, doctrine or dogma of their religion.

The Lord Jesus Christ taught in Mark 7:6-9, *Well hath Esaias prophesied of you hypocrites, as it is written, This people honoureth me with their lips, but their _____ is far from me. Howbeit in vain do they worship me, teaching for doctrines the commandments of _____. For laying aside the commandment of God, ye hold the tradition of men, as the washing of pots and cups: and many other such like things ye do. And he said unto them, Full well ye reject the commandment of God, that ye may keep your own tradition.* God does not accept the traditions of men.

2. The only true source of authority is the Word of God.

In Matthew 7:13-14, Jesus Christ taught that the only way which truly leads men to God is through Himself: *Enter ye in at the strait gate: for wide is the gate, and broad is the way, that leadeth to destruction, and many there be which go in thereat: Because strait is the gate, and narrow is the _____, which leadeth unto life, and _____ there be that find it.* So that there be no doubt as to **the only way to God**, Jesus declared in John 14:6: *I am the _____, the truth, and the life: _____ man cometh unto the Father, but by me.*

In view of the fact that Satan is the great deceiver, he has introduced his teachings, wanting us to believe that the "broad way" also leads to Heaven. The devil always twists and distorts the Word of God. The Apostle Peter declared in 2nd Peter 3:16 that the false teachers were distorting and twisting the Word of God that the Apostle Paul had communicated to the churches: *As also in all his epistles, speaking in them of these things; in which are some things hard to be understood, which they that are _____ and unstable wrest [twist], as they do also the other Scriptures, unto their own destruction.* This happened primarily because they did not know the Lord Jesus Christ as their Savior and could not understand these spiritual truths. The Apostle Paul explains this in 1st Corinthians 2:12-14: *Now we have received, not the _____ of the world, but the _____ which is of God; that we might know the things that are freely given to us of God. Which things also we speak, not in the words which man's wisdom teacheth, but which the Holy Ghost teacheth; comparing spiritual things with spiritual.* [This refers to comparing passages in the Word of God with different passages in the Word of God.] *But the natural man receiveth not the things of the Spirit of God: for they are foolishness unto him: neither can he know them, because they are spiritually discerned.*

The majority of religions teach that there is life after death (the eternal existence of the soul and spirit), but only the Bible teaches that there is eternal life in the presence of God for true believers in Jesus Christ as their Savior. This eternal life with Jesus Christ is a real and tangible life with body, soul and spirit. The Apostle Paul warns in Colossians 2:8, *Beware lest any man spoil you through philosophy and vain deceit, after the _____ of men, after the rudiments of the world, and not after Christ.* Many sincere

44

people have a system of beliefs, but do not know or understand what it is to have a close fellowship with Jesus Christ; and much less can they comprehend what eternal life is with Him. Carefully examine your heart with the following questions:

a. Is your faith based on your intelligence?_____ The mind of man **cannot be the ultimate judge of Truth.** (Romans 1:21-22)

b. Is your faith based on experiences? _____ The activities and experiences of man **cannot be the concluding source of Truth.** (2nd Peter 1:16-21)

c. Is your faith based on religious traditions? _____ Religious rites, rituals, customs and traditions **cannot draw us to God. Our faith can only be based upon the authority of God's Word.** (Mark 7:6-9; Colossians 2:8)

II. GOD GAVE HIS PLAN, BUT MAN DISTORTED IT.

Read John 8:39-47.

1. What opinion did these people have about their relationship with God? _____
   _____

2. Was God their father? _____

3. Who was their father? _____

4. Because one believes that God is his Father, does that make it so? _____ How do you know this is true? _____
   _____

5. How can we know that God is really our Father? (Matthew 7:21) _
   _____
   _____

7. There are only two families (two fathers) in the world. Who are they?

   a. Family of _____ (1 John 3:1-3)

   b. Family of _____ (John 8:42-44)

8. There are many who do not want to hear the Word of God. Why? ___

_____

_____

Read Genesis 2:7, 21-22.

9. Is God the creator of Adam and Eve? _____

10. Could God create man with sinful tendencies? _____

11. When Adam and Eve sinned, did they receive a sin nature? _____

12. Because we are descendants of Adam and Eve, they are our ancestors. Have we received from them their sinful nature? _____ This is clearly taught in Romans 5:12: *Wherefore, as by* _____ *man sin entered into the world, and death by sin; and so death* _____ *upon all men, for that all have sinned.*

13. There is a vast difference between God, the Creator and parents, who procreate!

    a. The Creator made man perfect with no sinful tendencies.

    b. The parents have received a God-given capability to have children, but since the parents are sinners, their children also receive that sinful nature.

14. Why did the children of Adam and Eve have to be born with a sinful nature? _____

_____

_____

_____

III. GOD EXPLAINED THE NECESSITY OF HAVING A NEW BIRTH.

Read John 3:1-10.

1. What do we know about Nicodemus? He was a _____, a _____ of the Jews, and he came to Jesus at _____.

2. Being a strict Jewish religious leader, what did he think was necessary to be able to enter Heaven? _____

3. What prerequisite did Jesus teach Nicodemus to be able to enter into the kingdom of God? _____

4. What were the two sarcastic questions that Nicodemus directed to Jesus? (John 3:4)_____

   _____

5. The spiritual birth of which Jesus spoke had two factors. Without them it is impossible to be saved. What are they? (John 3:5) They have to be born of _____ and of the _____

6. To help Nicodemus understand more clearly, Jesus Christ spoke of two different types of births. We see this in John 3:6. What are they? _____ and _____ We should not confuse the two types of births. The one is totally physical, and the other is totally the work of God.

7. In many parts of the Bible, *water* refers to the Word of God. It does not refer to physical water. What does this "water" refer to in John 3:5? _____

8. In John 4:7-14, Jesus carefully explained that He was not talking about physical water. To what class of water was he referring? _____

   _____

9. Ephesians 5:26 declares that the Christian is sanctified and cleansed *with the washing of water by the* _____.

10. James 1:18 and 1ˢᵗ Peter 1:23 talk about a new birth by the _____

    _____.

11. Throughout these passages we see that the "water" is the _____

    _____.

12. In John 3:3 and 7, Jesus Christ helps us to clearly see that it is essential for us to be _____ again so that we can enter into the Kingdom of God.

13. This new birth takes place by means of "water," which is the _____ of God and by the work of the Holy Spirit.

14. The Holy _____ uses the Word of God to bring understanding, knowledge, conviction, repentance and faith to the sinner.

15. According to John 8:44-47, to whom do all those belong who have only experienced the first birth? _____ According to John 3:3, to whom do those people belong who have experienced their second birth (spiritual)? _____

16. Is it possible to enter into the Kingdom of God having only experienced the first birth? _____ Why? _____
_____

17. What is the difference between the new birth and being reformed? The new birth is totally the transforming work of _____, which is eternal. Being reformed is achieved through the efforts of _____, which only results in a temporal change.

18. Is it possible that a person can reform his sinful nature enough to be able to enter Heaven by his good works? _____ How? _____
_____

IV. WE HAVE TO BECOME SONS OF GOD.

1. John 1:12 clearly expresses the necessity *to become the sons of God*. This happens when we **repent** of our sins and **surrender** (give ourselves) to Jesus Christ with all our heart. He saves us and comes to live within us from that moment on. He receives us as members of His family, giving us the *power* (authority) *to become the sons of God*. Ephesians 2:8-9 teaches: *For by grace are ye saved through faith; and **that not of yourselves**: it is the gift of God: Not of _____, lest any man should boast.* It is the "grace of God" and the "faith that come from God" that enables us to fully trust in the Lord Jesus Christ as our Savior. This is what He did for us by taking our punishment when He died on the cross and shed His blood for us.

2. John 1:13 declares that it is impossible to become a son of God by being born into our earthly family: *Which were born, **not of blood**.* In other words, being born into a Christian family does not make one a Christian, any more than if your father, being a carpenter would make you a carpenter. Salvation does not come through family heritage. True salvation does not take place through a physical birth, but through a _____ one.

3. In John 1:13 Jesus Christ affirms that to become a son of God is **not *of the will of the flesh.*** He is teaching that the **new birth** is not

something you can achieve through your own efforts by good works or personal reform. God has to do the work by His authority and power. It is not the result of your works and personal reform.

4. John 1:13 continues by saying, *nor of the will of man*. It is teaching that the **new birth** is not something that another person can do for you. It does not come through baptism, confirmation, religious rituals or rites. God has to do the work.

5. The only solution for the lost condition of mankind is completely beyond our human capabilities. John 1:13 declares that it is only by the *grace of God* (His unmerited favor) that we can be saved. God has to do the work of saving us. There is **NOTHING** that we can do of ourselves to be saved. We can teach them, warn them, and give them the Gospel message; however, we cannot force them to repent of their sin and deposit their trust in Jesus Christ as their Savior! True faith only comes through God's Word and God has to bring conviction and a true repentance for sin.

V. GOD PROVIDED THE OPPORTUNITY FOR SALVATION.

1. Through a miracle, God the Second Person of the Trinity, received a human body, and the virgin Mary gave birth to Jesus Christ. John 1:14 declares, *And the Word was made _____, and dwelt among us, (and we beheld his glory, the glory as of the only begotten of the Father,) full of grace and truth.* Jesus Christ was 100% man and at the same time 100% God.

2. Jesus Christ received upon Himself the sin of the whole world and gave Himself to die on the cross for all our sins. Peter explains in 1st Peter 3:18, *For Christ also hath once suffered for _____, the just for the unjust, that he might bring us to God.*

3. Jesus Christ physically arose from the dead after being in the tomb three days and three nights to assure us of eternal salvation, and to also guarantee that we will some day be resurrected from the dead. Romans 4:25 says, *Who was delivered for our offences, and was _____ again for our justification.* The Apostle Paul assured all Christians in 1st Corinthians 15:20, *But now is Christ **risen** from the dead, and become the firstfruits of them that slept.* Summing up these three great events, the Apostle John gives a way of testing

their teachings as to whether they are in agreement with sound doctrine. It declares in 1st John 4:2-3, *Hereby know ye the Spirit of God:* Every _____ *that confesseth that Jesus Christ is come in the* _____ *is of God: And every spirit that confesseth not that Jesus Christ is come in the flesh is not of God: and this is that spirit of antichrist, whereof ye have heard that it should come; and even now already is it in the world.* The word **spirit** refers to the **spirit of the teaching or the full meaning of the teaching**. It is **not** a reference to the Holy Spirit. Notice the many times that this passage mentions that ***Jesus Christ is come in the flesh.*** This refers to **His physical birth, His physical death and His physical resurrection**. Those who teach that Jesus Christ was not fully man and at the same time fully God, or that He did not physically die on the cross, was buried and physically arose from the dead are proclaiming the lie of the antichrist. This passage in John opposes the false teaching that the resurrection of Jesus Christ was only a spiritual one and not a physical one. Any teaching that is not in agreement with the Word of God must be rejected.

4. Jesus Christ is the **only Mediator** between God the Father and man. 1st Timothy 2:5-6 affirms, *For there is one God, and one Mediator between God and men, the man Christ Jesus; Who gave himself a ransom for all.* Here the term ***Mediator*** has reference to what Jesus Christ did when He paid the penalty for our sins, dying on the cross of Calvary. This passage confirms that Jesus Christ is the only Mediator (substitute) for man before God. **There is no other!**

SUMMARY:

Salvation is only based on what the Bible, the Word of God, says. No writing declared "sacred" or "infallible" by men can ever be equal or superior to the Bible. 2nd Peter 1:16-21 makes reference to those books as *cunningly devised fables* that try to appear similar to the Word of God, or they even minimize the Bible. The Apostle Peter expressed it this way: *For we have not followed cunningly devised fables, when we made known unto you the power and coming of our Lord Jesus Christ, but were eyewitnesses of his majesty. For he received from God the Father honour and glory, when there came such a voice to him from the excellent glory, This is my beloved Son, in whom I am well pleased. And this voice which came from Heaven we heard, when we were with him in the holy mount. We have also a more sure word of prophecy* [God's Word]; *whereunto ye do well that ye take heed, as unto a light that shineth in a dark place, until the day dawn, and the day star arise in your hearts: Knowing this first, that no prophecy of the Scripture is of any private interpretation. For the prophecy came not in old time by the will of man: but holy men of God spake as they were moved by the Holy Ghost.* This truth is also confirmed in 2nd Timothy 3:16-17: *All Scripture is given by inspiration of God, and is profitable for doctrine, for reproof, for correction, for instruction in righteousness: That the man of God may be perfect, thoroughly furnished unto all good works.*

If there was anything we could to do through our own efforts, like fulfilling religious rites, rituals, traditions, baptisms, confirmations or personal reforms, **then Jesus Christ would not have had to die for our sins.** Salvation only comes through the finished work of Jesus Christ when He died and arose from the dead. If salvation could be achieved by what we could offer God, such as our money, possessions or special sacrifices, then God would be unjust by not making the conditions for salvation within the reach of all mankind. God has provided only one plan for salvation whereby we can be saved and have fellowship with Him. Only those who truly repent of their sins, trust Jesus Christ as their personal Savior and give themselves to Him, can *become the sons of God.* (John 1:12)

REVIEW QUESTIONS – CHAPTER 4

WHO ARE THE SONS OF GOD?

Underline the correct answer: (True) or (False)

1. (True) or (False) God is the Father of all mankind.

2. (True) or (False) If you have an unusual experience you can know that you have been born again.

3. (True) or (False) No writings by religious men, which have been declared "sacred" or "infallible," can ever be equal or superior to the Bible. The Bible is the only inspired Word of God!

4. (True) or (False) Only two classes of people exist in the human race, those who belong to God and those who belong to Satan.

5. (True) or (False) True faith can only be based upon the authority of God's Word. (Romans 10:17)

6. (True) or (False) All human beings are sinners except for Jesus Christ.

7. (True) or (False) In the Bible, when "baptism" is mentioned, it always refers to baptism in water.

8. (True) or (False) Because Jesus Christ loves us, He became our substitute by taking the sins of the whole world upon Himself, and then He received the punishment from God the Father for our sins.

9. (True) or (False) God is the Father of all who claim to believe in Him.

10. (True) or (False) So God can become our Father, we have to be "born again" into His family.

11. (True) or (False) So that God can be our Father, we have to do many good works.

12. (True) or (False) Even though a person has not repented of his sins, if he fervently prays, God will save him.

13. (True) or (False) The moment we become sons of God, we receive a new nature that only God can give us. (2nd Corinthians 5:17-18)

14. (True) or (False) The new birth comes only through the Word of God by permitting the Holy Spirit to do His ministry in our heart. He convinces us of the need to repent of our sins and to give ourselves to Jesus Christ with all our heart.

15. (True) or (False) Many have been deceived by emotional experiences, which have made them believe they are saved.

16. (True) or (False) God accepts an emotional experience as proof of our salvation.

17. (True) or (False) All those who **say** they have accepted or received Jesus Christ as their Savior belong to God and are truly saved.

18. Please memorize John 1:11-12 and express it in your own words. _____
   _____
   _____
   _____

The next lesson helps us to understand what true salvation involves.

Chapter Five

Salvation: The Spiritual Birth

For by grace are ye saved through faith; and that not of yourselves:
it is the gift of God: Not of works, lest any man should boast.

Ephesians 2:8-9

ACCORDING TO GOD'S WORD, IN WHAT CONDITION DO WE FIND OURSELVES?

If a man had been shipwrecked in high seas without a lifesaver and at the point of drowning, what would he need? Would he need a few words of encouragement, a better job, more money, a new car, a better house or a doctor? Of course not! He would need someone that could save him from the danger of drowning. In the same way, the majority of the people in the world are in a lost condition and heading for an eternity without the knowledge of true salvation. This salvation can only be given by the Lord Jesus Christ. Many are looking for temporal and material things in which to trust. Unfortunately, they are not interested in the Word of God, nor desire to hear messages regarding spiritual things. They do not understand the gravity of their spiritual condition. According to Ephesians 2:1-3 they are _____ in their trespasses and sins.

I. WE ARE LOST AND CONDEMNED SINNERS.

1. Romans 3:10-18 says all mankind is lost and on their way to hell, as we have seen in previous lessons. In verses 10 and 11 God says, *There is _____ righteous, no, not one: There is none that understandeth, there is none that seeketh after God.* In light of this passage, we see that man is incapable of pleasing God with his life, because he is spiritually dead.

2. The Bible gives us the reason sinful mankind is under the judgment and condemnation of God. John 3:17-20 declares that Christ did not come to condemn us to eternal death, because we were already condemned! This passage states, *For God sent not His Son into the world to condemn the world; but that the world through him might be saved. He that believeth* [deposit all his confidence] *on him is not condemned: but he that believeth not is condemned _____, because he hath not believed in the name of the only begotten Son of God. And this is the condemnation, that light is come into the world, and men loved darkness rather than light, because their deeds were evil.*

3. How many people are guilty of being sinners? Romans 3:23 says, *For _____ have sinned, and come short of the glory of God.* This verse teaches that even the best person cannot reach God with his life or by his works, because he is sinful from the moment of his conception. With God there are no exceptions. 1ˢᵗ Peter 1:17 declares, *And if ye call on the Father, who without respect of persons judgeth according to every man's work.* We are all guilty sinners! Do you recognize that you are a terrible sinner and need to be saved? _____

4. The Bible tells us that eternal condemnation (eternal death) is only for lost sinners. This death is terrible. We should understand that the word, *death* has several meanings.

   a. **Physical death** refers to the separation of the soul and the spirit from the body. Upon physical death, our soul and spirit continue to live on in its eternal destiny.

   b. **Spiritual death** is the condition in which man finds himself without Christ. This is the part of man that died when Adam and Eve obeyed Satan, sinned against God and broke their fellowship with Him. Ephesians 2:1 speaks of the dead condition of the spirit of the individual before he trusts Jesus Christ as his Savior: *And you hath he quickened* [made alive], *who were dead in trespasses and sins.*

    c. Eternal death is the destiny of a person who dies physically without having placed his faith and confidence in Jesus Christ with all his heart as his Savior. The lost sinner is separated (soul, spirit and body) from God forever. This person goes to his eternal destiny without Christ. According to the Bible, he first goes to *Hell,* and after the final judgment, he goes to the *Lake of Fire.* This is not the destruction or annihilation of the soul. The spirit and soul man will never stop existing. This last class of death is what the Bible calls "eternal condemnation" or "eternal death." This is explained in Revelation 20:11-15.

    Romans 6:23 makes clear that the result or *the wages of sin is **death**.* To what kind of death does this refer? _____

    In contrast, the moment that the true Christian dies, his soul and spirit go directly to Heaven with Jesus Christ. The Apostle Paul confirmed this in 2nd Corinthians 5:8: *absent from the body, and to be* _____ *with the Lord.* Philippians 1:21 stated, *For to me to live is Christ, and to die is gain.* The Apostle Paul declared in verse 23, *For I am in a strait betwixt two, having a desire to depart, and to be with Christ; which is far better.* This promise was given only to those who know the Lord Jesus Christ as their personal Savior.

5. In Isaiah 64:6, God declares that all of us are wicked and terrible sinners: *But we are* _____ *as an unclean thing, and all* _____ *righteousnesses are as filthy rags; and we all do fade as a leaf; and our iniquities* [sins], *like the wind, have taken us away.* How do you see your own good works? _____
According to the authority of the Bible, how does God see your good works? _____ Do you recognize that you are a lost sinner and in need of salvation? _____

II. WE ARE UNABLE TO SAVE OURSELVES.

1. James 2:10 teaches, *For whosoever shall keep the whole law, and yet offend in* _____ *point, he is* _____ *of all.* We are in a spiritual dilemma! Mankind is incapable of fulfilling the perfection that God requires. If it were possible to be saved by fulfilling the

Law of God, we would have to completely obey **all of the Law.**

2. Ephesians 2:8-9 declares that only God can save us: *For by grace are ye saved through faith; and that not of* _____: *it is the gift of God: **not of works**, lest any man should boast.* Many try to gain salvation by their works, attending church, fulfilling certain religious rites and rituals, making large contributions, or just being a good citizen. They endeavor to be good, loving and respectful people in order to gain favor with God. They are deceived, believing that their good works can save them. Can any of these things save them? _____

3. 1st Corinthians 2:14 helps us to comprehend the reason so many do not understand the basic principles given in God's Word for salvation. It clearly states, *But the natural man receiveth* _____ *the things of the Spirit of God: for they are foolishness unto him: neither can he know them, because they are spiritually discerned.* Through his own efforts, he cannot improve his "old nature," or produce in himself a "new nature." His choices are determined by his personal desires. Man willingly makes choices that flow from the heart and acts in accordance with his sinful nature (James 1:13-15). In his fallen state, man cannot choose to be righteous. Both repentance and faith come through the Word of God by the working of the Holy Spirit in his life. When a person turns to Christ to surrender himself, he does so by the convicting power of God.

III. GOD LOVES US AND WANTS TO SAVE US.

1. In spite of our rebellion and sin, God loves us. What is the principal proof of **His love**? Romans 5:8 says, *But God commendeth His* _____ *toward us, in that, while we were yet sinners, Christ died for us.* By His teachings and revelations throughout the entire Bible, God shows His great love to all mankind. Do you know that God loves you? _____ How does He show that love to you? _____

The will and supreme desire of God is that no one should perish and go to the Lake of Fire for all eternity. Jesus Christ has done all that is necessary to save the sinner from condemnation. 2nd Peter 3:9 says, *The Lord is not slack concerning His promise, as some men count slackness; but is long-suffering to us-ward, not* _____ *that any should perish, but that all should come to repentance.* Furthermore, 1st Timothy 2:4 assures us that God would *have all men to be* _____, *to come unto the knowledge of the truth.* God does not want you to die without receiving His provision for eternal life. Do you understand that God is patiently waiting for you? _____

2. In spite of our sinful nature, God wants to save us by **His grace**. Ephesians 2:8 declares, *For by grace are ye saved through faith; and that* _____ *of yourselves: it is the gift of God.* **Grace** is a gift or a special consideration from God that we do not deserve. Romans 5:20-21 explains, *where sin abounded, grace did much more abound. That as sin hath reigned unto death, even so might grace reign through righteousness unto eternal life by Jesus Christ our Lord.* This gift of God cost the Lord Jesus Christ the great price of suffering death on the cross for our sins. He received the terrible judgment of God in our place. The whole plan of salvation is a revelation of the grace of God. Do you understand that even though you do not deserve anything, God wants to show you His grace? _____

3. If it were not for the **mercy of God** all of us would go to Hell, because this is the punishment that we deserve for our sins. In reality, we all deserve eternal condemnation in the Lake of Fire as mentioned in Revelation 20:15. The word, ***mercy*** means – "God does **not** give to us what we deserve." Psalm 103:8 shows the character of God: *The Lord is merciful and gracious, slow to anger, and plenteous in mercy.* Ephesians 2:4-5 declares, *But God, who is rich in* _____, *for His great love wherewith he loved us, even when we were dead in sins, hath quickened us* [made us alive] *together with Christ, (by grace ye are saved).* Also, James 5:11 affirms, *The Lord is very pitiful, and of tender* _____. Do you understand that even though you merit eternal damnation, God wants to show you His mercy? _____

IV. JESUS CHRIST IS THE PROVISION OF GOD FOR OUR SALVATION.

1. God gave us His only Son to show His great love for us. John 3:16 says, *For God so* _____ *the world* [you and me]*, that he gave His only begotten Son, that whosoever believeth in him should not perish, but have everlasting life.* The word, *believe* is the act of putting your complete confidence in Jesus Christ for salvation.

2. Jesus Christ took our place, suffered and died on the cross for us, taking upon Himself all of our sin. The prophecy in Isaiah 53:6

clearly describes what Jesus Christ did for us: *All we like sheep have gone astray; we have turned every one to his own way; and the Lord hath laid on _____ the iniquity* [sins] *of us all.* God the Father poured out His wrath upon Jesus Christ. He shed His blood on the cross and was punished in our place in payment for all sins. Even though salvation is a gift from God, the supreme price had to be paid. Do you recognize that the death of Jesus Christ shows how terrible God considers all of your sins? _____

3. Jesus Christ died on the cross, was buried in a tomb, and after three days physically arose from the dead. This assures us that He has the power to save us and cleanse us from all wickedness. In brief, this is the glorious and victorious message of the Gospel of the Lord Jesus Christ. This message was proclaimed by the Apostle Paul in 1ˢᵗ Corinthians 15:3-4: *For I delivered unto you first of all that which I also received, how that Christ _____ for our sins according to the Scriptures; and that he was _____, and that he _____ again the third day according to the Scriptures.* It is essential to believe in the physical resurrection of Jesus Christ; otherwise, it would be impossible to have the assurance of salvation. Are you convinced of the physical resurrection of our Lord Jesus Christ? _____

4. During the forty days following His resurrection, Jesus Christ ministered to His disciples and hundreds of other believers. In their presence the Lord Jesus Christ physically ascended to Heaven and sat down at the right hand of God the Father. He is the only mediator between God and man. The Apostle Paul teaches in 1ˢᵗ Timothy 2:5, *there is one God, and one mediator between God and men, the man Christ Jesus.* This clearly means that He mediated between God and us for our sins. In verse 6, he explains the reason Jesus Christ is the **only mediator**: *Who gave himself a ransom for all, to be testified in due time.* We should not be confused between the words "intercessor" and "mediator." In this case the word, *mediator* indicates that only Jesus Christ could provide salvation for us by His death and resurrection. An *intercessor* is a person who intercedes for another. In Romans 8:26, we learn that the Holy Spirit intercedes for us, but only the Lord Jesus Christ can be the mediator between God and man.

V. GOD'S PLAN OF SALVATION IS MADE CLEAR.

The foundation of our salvation is the Word of God. We need to firmly believe that the Bible is the only inspired and authoritative Word of God. Hebrews 1:1-3 states, *God, who at sundry times and in divers* [diverse or different] *manners spake in time past unto the fathers* [referring to the Jews of the Old Testament], *by the prophets hath in these last days spoken unto us by his _____, whom he hath appointed heir of all things, by whom also he made the worlds; Who being the brightness of his glory, and the express image of his person, and upholding all things by the word of his power, when he had by himself purged our sins, sat down on the right hand of the Majesty on high.* The Apostle Paul clearly teaches in 1ˢᵗ Thessalonians 2:13 that the Word of God was not the innovation of men, but God spoke directly to men: *For this cause also thank we God without ceasing, because, when ye received the word of God which ye heard of us, ye received it not as the word of men, but as it is in truth, the Word of God, which effectually worketh also in you that believe.* How did we receive this wonderful treasure? Again the Apostle Paul gave the answer in 2ⁿᵈ Timothy 3:16: *All Scripture is given by inspiration of _____, and is profitable for doctrine, for reproof, for correction, for instruction in righteousness.*

God's plan for salvation includes the following six basic principles:

1. Receive the "faith of Jesus Christ."

Many feel that they have a great faith created and promoted by their own will or through their religion; however, we are **not** saved by **our own faith**, by what we do or what we are. If it is not our faith, then how are we to be saved? God declares that it is impossible for our own faith to save us. According to God's Word, **it is only the faith that the Lord Jesus Christ imparts to us that enables us to truly place our full confidence in Him**. Galatians 2:16 declares that the justification that God gives us is not because of the good works that we might have done, or by our own faith, but by the faith of Jesus Christ: *Knowing that a man is _____ justified by the works of the law, but by the faith of Jesus Christ, even we have believed in Jesus Christ, that we might be justified by the faith of Christ, and _____ by the works of the law: for by the works of the law shall no flesh be justified.*

It is first necessary to hear the Word of God to be able to believe

59

God. Romans 10:17 insists that this faith is not our faith, but the faith that comes through the Word of God: *So then _____ cometh by hearing, and hearing by the Word of God.* In Romans 4:3, the Apostle Paul spoke of the salvation of Abraham in the Old Testament and how he received God's righteousness: *Abraham believed God, and it was _____ unto him for righteousness.* God gave him this special faith to believe. As the result of Abraham placing his trust completely in God, he was declared righteous or right before God.

We believe God for what He says in His Word and for what He did for us; therefore, we must place our complete faith and confidence in Jesus Christ, God the Son, for what He did through His death and resurrection. This signifies that this faith can **only** come from Jesus Christ through the Word of God. For whom did Jesus do this? _____ Now, answer it with your name. Jesus Christ died for_____!

2. **Recognize that you are a terrible sinner.**

Because of our sin, it is necessary to recognize and admit our lost condition. We were born sinners; therefore, we have a sinful nature. God sees us as we are, vile and terrible sinners, as declared in Romans 3:10-18: *As it is written, There is none _____, no, not one: There is none that understandeth, there is none that seeketh after God. They are all gone out of the way, they are together become unprofitable; there is none that doeth good, no, not one. Their throat is an open sepulchre; with their tongues they have used deceit; the poison of asps is under their lips: Whose mouth is full of cursing and bitterness: Their feet are swift to shed blood: Destruction and misery are in their ways: And the way of peace have they not known: There is no fear of God before their eyes.* If there exists any doubt regarding this teaching, study once again chapters two and three. Read carefully Romans 3:23 and James 2:10. How does God see you?_____

3. **Repent of all your sin.**

The death of Jesus Christ completely paid our debt to God, but only a few will receive the forgiveness for their sin. Why? Because Jesus Christ said that we have to sincerely repent of our sin and trust in Him with all our heart. Jesus preached repentance from the beginning of His ministry. He said in Mark 1:15, *the time is fulfilled, and the kingdom of God is at hand: repent ye, and believe the Gospel.* The *Gospel* includes what Jesus Christ did for us in His life, death, burial and resurrection. Jesus Christ gave the order to first **repent** and then to **believe the Gospel.** As we examine the meaning of repentance, we will understand what it involves, the purpose for it, and how it should affect our life before and after our conversion. In Luke 3:8, John the Baptist commanded, *Bring forth therefore _____ worthy of repentance.* In other words, "Prove by your actions your sincere sorrow for your sin." Some teach that repentance is a work or human effort that has been added to God's plan for the purpose of achieving salvation. That is not true! The Apostle Paul confronts us with a question in Romans 2:4, *Or despisest thou the riches of his goodness and forbearance and longsuffering; not knowing that the _____ of God leadeth thee to repentance?* The Holy Spirit uses the Word of God in our heart and life to convict us of sin bringing us to repentance. We must obey God's command to repent with all our heart!

What is true repentance? True repentance is the change in our way of thinking: toward sin, toward God, toward ourselves and toward the world and a worldly life.

a. **Repentance is a change in our way of thinking toward sin.** It is a change in our attitudes toward sin with the purpose of recognizing it, and judging it for what it is, evil and terrible. In Luke 24:47, Jesus insisted *that repentance and remission of sins should be _____ in his name among all nations, beginning at Jerusalem.* Throughout the Bible, the servants of God wrote and preached regarding the necessity of true repentance for the forgiveness of sin. True repentance is not part of faith, but comes to us in the same way as faith, by the Word of God. Mark 1:4 states, *John did baptize in the wilderness, and preach the _____ of repentance for the remission of sins.* What does **baptism of repentance** mean? The word, **baptism,** used here has nothing to do with water, but emphatically teaches that we have to be completely submersed in repentance. It clearly teaches that repentance was necessary for the forgiveness of sins. Matthew 3:6-8 says they *were baptized of him in Jordan, confessing their _____. But when he saw many of the Pharisees and Sadducees* *come to his baptism, he said unto them, O generation of vipers, who hath warned you to flee from the wrath to come? Bring forth therefore fruits meet for repentance.* This passage clearly teaches the importance of having a tangible evidence of true repentance.

b. **Repentance is a change in our way of thinking toward God**. A key factor of repentance has to do with your attitudes. Your attitudes of indifference and rebellion toward God have to change. Mark 12:30 commands, *thou shalt _____ the Lord thy God with all thy heart, and with all thy soul, and with all thy mind, and with all thy strength: this is the first commandment.* In Exodus 20:2-5, God gave this great and eternal commandment to a people who did not really love Him: *I am the Lord thy God, which have brought thee out of the land of Egypt, out of the house of bondage. Thou shalt have no other _____ before me. Thou shalt not make unto thee any graven image, or any likeness of any thing that is in Heaven above, or that is in the earth beneath, or that is in the water under the earth. Thou shalt not bow down thyself to them, nor serve them: for I the Lord thy God am a jealous God, visiting the iniquity of the fathers upon the children unto the third and fourth generation of them that hate me.* It is a terrible chain of judgment, which can only be terminated when a person loves and obeys God. We must not forget what Jesus declared in John 14:21, *He that hath my commandments, and keepeth them, he it is that loveth me: and he that loveth me shall be loved of my Father, and I will love him, and will manifest myself to him.* Do you love your sin and your religion, or do you love the Lord Jesus Christ for who He is and what He has done for you? _____

c. **Repentance is a change in our way of thinking toward ourselves.** We have to understand that the death of Jesus Christ completely paid our debt with God, but just because it is paid does not mean that we have received His forgiveness or pardon. The Lord Jesus gave the command in Luke 13:24, _____ *to enter in at the strait gate.* The word, ***strive*** in Greek is "agonize," which denotes nothing less than **true repentance** on our part. It is a change of our attitudes regarding what we are and the way we live. Repentance causes us to humble ourselves before Almighty God. Job 42:6 is a good example of a genuine sadness produced by God: *Wherefore I abhor myself, and _____ in dust and ashes.*

God wants to cleanse us of all our wickedness and sin, but if a person is rebellious and does not want to be cleansed, or if he has no desire to leave his sins God cannot save him. If you desire, love, or practice your sinful habits, it is idolatry, which is an abomination to God. The Bible says that if you love your sins you do not love God! God emphatically declares that there is no agreement between God and this worldly system. The Apostle John is explicit in 1st John 3:8, *He that committeth* [practice] *sin is of the* _____; *for the devil sinneth from the beginning.* The crucial word in this verse is ***practices,*** indicating a love and desire for sin. Can the Word of God cause us to change our attitudes toward our personal desires and bring us to true repentance? Yes!

The only valid repentance comes directly or indirectly through the Word of God. There are many who grieve and shed tears over the **consequences of their sin**, but that is not true repentance. There needs to be sincere hatred for the sin. Please read the important passage in 2nd Corinthians 7:8-10 where the Apostle Paul explains the difference between a normal sadness and a sadness that is produced by God: *For though I made you sorry with a letter, I do not repent, though I did repent* [I was saddened]: *for I perceive that the same epistle hath made you sorry, though it were but for a season. Now I rejoice, not that ye were made sorry, but that ye sorrowed to* _____: *for ye were made sorry after a godly manner, that ye might receive damage by us in nothing. For godly sorrow worketh repentance to salvation not to be repented of: but the sorrow of the world worketh death.* This passage teaches that they received true repentance through the Word of God and were forgiven. In Acts 3:19, the Apostle Peter helps you to understand that after you truly repent, true conversion takes place when you give yourself to Jesus Christ: *Repent ye therefore, and be converted, that your* _____ *may be blotted out, when the times of refreshing shall come from the presence of the Lord.* Can you have true repentance only because you regret something or feel sadness for some terrible sin? _____

d. **True repentance is a change in our heart toward the world and a worldly life**. Our attitudes toward this worldly system and the practice of sin have to change. 1st John 2:15 gives emphasis to this truth saying: *Love not the world, neither the things that*

63

*are in the world. If any man love the world, **the _____ of the Father is not in him.*** In 2nd Corinthians 6:14-18, the Apostle Paul repeats an important command from the Old Testament to all who belong to God: *Be ye not unequally yoked together with _____: for what fellowship hath righteousness with unrighteousness? and what communion* [fellowship] *hath light with darkness? And what concord hath Christ with Belial? or what part hath he that believeth with an infidel? And what agreement hath the temple of God with idols? for ye are the temple of the living God; as God hath said, I will dwell in them, and walk in them; and I will be their God, and they shall be my people. Wherefore come out from among them, and be ye separate, saith the Lord, and touch not the unclean thing; and I will receive you. And will be a Father unto you, and ye shall be my sons and daughters, saith the Lord Almighty.* How can a person love God and at the same time love worldly practices? It is a contradiction!

e. **What will happen to those who do not repent of their sin with all their heart?** Repentance is essential in order to receive true salvation. Sadly, many pastors teach that repentance is unnecessary in order to receive the forgiveness of sins. It is a terrible error! In reference to true repentance, 2nd Peter 3:9 declares, *The Lord is not slack concerning his promise, as some men count slackness; but is longsuffering to us-ward, not willing that any should perish but that all should come to _____.* Many live with a false security having made a superficial decision "to accept or receive Jesus Christ as their Savior." They are actually void of a correct understanding as to what true salvation involves. Such an action is referred to as "easy-believism," which results in only a verbal "profession of faith." Almost all of Christianity uses the expression, "accept or receive Jesus Christ as their Savior," but they all mean something different. This terminology has become ambiguous. **We cannot suppose that a person understands what true salvation involves just because he uses common terminology.** It is possible for you to believe and accept the facts and data about Jesus Christ, and at the same time not be saved. If somebody makes a "profession of faith" with the purpose of only avoiding eternal punishment, he is deceiving himself. It demonstrates that he does not understand what God teaches about true repentance and true faith.

64

The Apostle Paul asks the following important question in Romans 2:4: *Despisest thou the riches of his goodness and forbearance and longsuffering* [patience]*; not knowing that the goodness of _____ leadeth thee to repentance?* The Apostle Paul continues his serious accusation against them in Romans 2:5-6, for the hardness of their heart and their rejection of God's goodness: *But after thy hardness and impenitent* [non repented] *heart treasurest up unto thyself _____* [anger] *against the day of wrath and revelation of the righteous judgment of God; Who will render to every man according to his deeds.* Carefully read again 2nd Corinthians 7:10: *For godly sorrow worketh repentance to salvation not to be repented of: but the sorrow of the world worketh* ***death***. The *death* mentioned here refers to eternal death. Revelation 20:11-15 teaches that they will receive the punishment of God for their sin in "Hell," and later appear before the "Great White Throne Judgment" where they will be condemned to the "Lake of Fire" for all eternity.

4. **Believe with all your heart**

The word ***believe*** is often used in our everyday vocabulary in several different ways. First, we have a historical belief of things that happened in the past. The use of the biblical word, *believe*, imports a much greater meaning than just a simple recognition of facts and truths. The problem that many people have is that they only believe historical facts about the Bible and the Lord Jesus Christ.

Second, we often use the word, *believe* in reference to doubtful situations. For example, we might express doubt as to whether or not we think or believe that it might rain today, etc. Unfortunately, many treat basic biblical truths with uncertain belief. They are in reality doubting God's Word.

The third use of the word, *believe*, which is found in the Bible, denotes a positive and complete trust. In Greek, the language in which the New Testament was written, we see that the word, *believe* is the act of **"completely depositing your trust and confidence in someone or something."** We must deposit our complete confidence in what God says in His Word. 1st John 5:10 says, *He that believeth on the Son of God hath the witness in himself: he that believeth _____ God, hath made Him a liar; because he believeth _____* *the record that God gave of His Son.* Those who do not believe God's Word are actually declaring that God is a liar.

Give careful attention to what Jesus said in John 3:18: *He that _____ on him* [Jesus Christ] *is not condemned: but he that believeth not is condemned already, because he hath not believed in the name of the only begotten Son of God.* Have you truly deposited your confidence in what the Word of God says? _____
It is imperative to believe with all your heart (in the deepest part of your being) that Jesus Christ shed His blood and died on the cross to take the punishment for your sins, and after three days he physically arose in order to save you. Along with true repentance, the Apostle Paul declares in Romans 10:9-10, *That if thou shalt confess with thy mouth the Lord Jesus, and shalt _____* **in thine heart** *that God hath raised him from the dead, thou shalt be saved. For with the heart man believeth unto righteousness; and with the mouth confession is made unto salvation.* This is not just a head-knowledge, but an act of fully trusting in Jesus Christ as your personal Savior by giving yourself to Him. Jesus Christ took upon Himself the punishment that we deserve. He is our substitute. This enables us to come into true fellowship with Him and have His help in our daily life. Besides taking your place to free you from eternal punishment, He wants to forgive all of your sins and give you a new life.

5. **Ask God to forgive your sins.**

With all sincerity, we have to ask God in prayer to forgive us for our sins through Jesus Christ. In Luke 18:13, we read about a publican, who was praying in the temple, feeling a profound repentance for his sin: *And the publican standing afar off, would not lift up so much as his eyes unto Heaven, but smote upon his breast, saying, God be _____ to me a sinner.* He asked God for forgiveness with a contrite (repentant) heart, and God forgave his sin. If you ask Him with a truly repentant heart, God will forgive you and cleanse you from all your sin.

Do you have a change in your thinking and attitudes regarding yourself and your life? _____ Do you recognize your sin for what it is, bad and terrible? _____ Do you have a true change in your heart toward God, and a genuine sadness for the sins that you have committed? _____ God wants to cleanse you from all sin. 1st John

1:9-10 reminds us, *If we confess* [to Jesus Christ] *our sins, he is faithful and just to _____ us our sins, and to cleanse us from all unrighteousness. If we say that we have not sinned, we make him a liar, and his truth is not in us.* If you do not want to be cleansed, or if you love your sin and do not want to abandon it, **can God do a work in your life against your will?** _____ Can God save you when your love is directed toward what God hates? _____ Do you love what God hates and hate what God loves? _____ If you love the sin that God hates, will God ignore your willful rejection? _____

6. **Give yourself with all your heart to Jesus Christ.**

Besides many other passages in the Bible, we read in 1st Corinthians 6:19-20 that we **become the property of God**, belonging to Him forever. The Apostle Paul asked, *What? know ye not that your body is the temple of the Holy Ghost which is in you, which ye have of God and ye are not your _____? For ye are _____ with a price: therefore glorify God in your body, and in your spirit, which are God's.* This verse teaches that **we must give ourselves to Jesus Christ. It is a commitment for the rest of our life**! When I gave myself to Jesus Christ I no longer belonged to myself. I do not want to participate in the worldly things that I did before, but now I want to obey the Lord Jesus Christ and do His will. The Apostle Paul confirms this in Galatians 2:20: *I am crucified with Christ: nevertheless I live; yet not I, but Christ liveth in me: and the life which I now live in the flesh I _____ by the faith of the Son of God, who loved me, and gave himself for me.* **We give ourselves to Jesus Christ, not out of obligation, but out of love for Him.** If you belong to Jesus Christ, then you will want to live according to His will and be obedient to God's Word. When we give ourselves to Jesus Christ we become His _____.

Romans 6:17 explains what happens when a person gives himself to Jesus Christ with all of his heart. The Apostle Paul declared, *But God be thanked, that ye were the servants of sin, but ye have obeyed from the heart that form of doctrine which was delivered you* [to whom you have given yourself]. Jesus Christ is the central figure of all Bible doctrine. Because of this, it has to be your own decision to give yourself to Jesus Christ so that He will be the center of your life forever. There is only one of two persons who can have control over your life,

Jesus Christ or Satan. To whom do you belong? _____

God demands our direct obedience to Christ with all our heart. Romans 6:18 continues, *Being then made free from sin, ye became the servants of righteousness.* We serve Him when we truly belong to Him. Please take time to analyze the fact that a "profession of faith," or just professing to belong to Jesus Christ, will not save you!

True faith in Jesus Christ as our Lord and Savior comes from God through the Word of God. The Holy Spirit of God guides us to believe and trust in Jesus Christ and causes us to react correctly. **This action of faith in Jesus Christ will result in true repentance for your sin, and the giving of yourself completely to Him. Jesus Christ has to have first place in your life. Can this happen by being religious? No! Can someone else make this decision for you? No!** This is your decision, not to be made by another. Children cannot do it for their parents, or their parents for their children. You must make this decision yourself! It is important to read God's Word, attend Bible studies, and hear God's Word faithfully preached in church services so that God can do His work in your heart. Do you remember how we receive true faith? The Apostle Paul gives the answer in Romans 10:17: *So then faith cometh by hearing and hearing by the Word of God.* The Bible is the instrument that God uses to enable you to understand His true plan of salvation.

VI. IS IT POSSIBLE TO BE A SECRET BELIEVER?

Is it possible for someone to repent of all his sins, to give himself to Christ with all his heart, to love Him with all his being, and at the same time secretly be a true Christian? _____ Matthew 10:32-33 says, *Whosoever therefore shall _____ me before men, him will I confess also before my Father which is in Heaven. But whosoever shall deny me before men, him will I also deny before my Father which is in Heaven.* Here the word *confess* means – "the act of giving testimony before others that we belong to Jesus Christ." It is difficult to understand why someone would not be willing to renounce his old life and give testimony to others of his new life in Christ. We realize there are pressures that come from the family, religious organizations, society, the work place, and at times the government, but never can a cowardly attitude be justified on the part of a true believer. When we trust the Lord Jesus Christ as our personal Savior we must never deny Him to the world around us. Upon reading John 12:42-43, we understand that God requires fearlessness as we witness regarding our faith in Jesus Christ: *Nevertheless among the chief rulers also many believed on him; but because of the Pharisees they did not _____ him, lest they should be put out of the synagogue: for they loved the praise of men more than the praise of God.* What occurred in the times of Jesus Christ, also happens today with those who secretly profess to be Christians, but will not give a solid testimony for fear of being rejected by society. In Romans 1:16, we see exactly the opposite with the Apostle Paul: *For I am not _____ of the Gospel of Christ: for it is the power of God unto salvation to every one that believeth.* Romans 10:9-11 shows the attitude of a true Christian: *That if thou shalt _____ with thy mouth the Lord Jesus, and shalt believe in thine heart that God hath raised him from the dead, thou shalt be saved. For with the heart man believeth unto righteousness; and with the mouth confession is made unto salvation. For the Scripture saith, Whosoever believeth on him **shall not be ashamed**.* Is it possible to be a true believer in Jesus Christ and at the same time to keep it as a secret? No! Why? _____

• **Do you really want to be a disciple of Jesus Christ?** _____

• **Please study carefully the following and consider the cost of being a true disciple of the Lord Jesus Christ.**

VII. IT COSTS A LOT TO BE A DISCIPLE OF JESUS CHRIST!

Jesus Christ paid the complete price so that you can be saved, but it will cost you dearly if you truly want to follow Him and be His disciple. It isn't logical for anyone to ever enter into a commitment or business transaction without first knowing the cost or the consequences of that commitment. Neither should you make a spiritual commitment without considering first what Jesus Christ said in Luke 14 about the trials and difficulties that will come to the true Christian. You should never make a promise to God if you do not intend to fulfill it or if you do not understand it. God holds you responsible for your decisions. Ignorance does not give us an excuse with God. The commitment to give yourself to Jesus Christ requires that you understand God's plan for salvation. It is not just a mere decision, a belief or a prayer, just because you think it is something good to do.

There are seven basic truths to help you understand the cost of being a true disciple of Jesus Christ. Salvation does not come through any of these seven basic truths; however, it is my desire to help you understand that there is a **cost for being a true disciple of the Lord Jesus Christ.**

1. **As a true disciple of Jesus Christ, your love and obedience to God has to be first.**

    Does your love for God take first place in your life? We are taught in Mark 12:30, *And thou shalt _____ the Lord thy God with all thy heart, and with all thy soul, and with all thy mind, and with all thy strength.* Can you love Christ in this way and continue to love images, traditions, relics, rituals or any other thing that you previously reverenced? If you trust in these things, the truth is, you do not love God. Deuteronomy 7:25 tells us what has to be done with these things: *The graven images of their gods shall ye _____ with fire: thou shalt not desire the silver or gold that is on them, nor take it unto thee, lest thou be snared therein: for it is an abomination* [hatred] *to the Lord thy God.* The Bible clearly teaches that anything that takes the place of God is idolatry. What does God hate? _____ What does God require that we do with those things? _____

    As a disciple of Jesus Christ, your attitudes will change toward worldliness and the world will change its way of treating you. What should be your attitude toward the world? 1st John 2:15-17 gives the answer: *Love not the _____, neither the things that are in the world. If any man love the _____, the love of the Father **is not in him**. For all that is in the world, the lust of the flesh, and the lust of the eyes, and the pride of life, is not of*

70

the Father, but is of the world. And the world passeth away, and the lust thereof: but he that doeth the will of God abideth forever. God hates worldly cravings and passions! It is not possible to continue in your old way of life and at the same time walk with God. Jesus Christ explained this to His disciples in John 15:18-20, *If the world hate you, ye know that it _____ me before it _____ you. If ye were of the world, the world would love his own: but because ye are not of the world, but I have chosen you out of the world, therefore the world hateth you. Remember the word that I said unto you, The servant is not greater than his lord. If they have persecuted me, they will also persecute you; if they have kept my saying, they will keep yours also.* The more fellowship we have with Jesus Christ, who is the LIGHT, the less we will be attracted to the darkness of this world. Jesus Christ declared in John 3:19, *And this is the condemnation, that light is come into the world, and men loved darkness rather than light, because their deeds were evil.*

2. **As a true disciple of Jesus Christ, you will have conflicts and at times divisions in your family because of the Gospel.**

   Read Luke 14:25-35. Verse 26 states, *If any man come to me, and _____ not his father, and mother, and wife, and children, and brethren, and sisters, yea, and his own life also, he cannot be my disciple.* What does it mean when Jesus said to "hate" your family? It does not mean that you should despise them, but that you love Jesus Christ more than your family. The love for your family should appear as if it were hatred in comparison to your great love for Jesus Christ. Our family members, parents, children, or in-laws are going to think that we are leaving the religion of which they approve. Christ knew that there would be conflicts in the family because of Him; therefore, you should not be surprised when you are rejected by them. For this reason, Jesus Christ insists that we give ourselves completely to Him. In Luke 12:51-53 and Matthew 10:34-38, Jesus warns us that *a man's foes shall be they of his own household.* When there is no true love in the home for Jesus Christ, those who belong to Him will often be rejected by the family. God does not want it this way! The believer can and must show even more love and patience for his family, because the love of Christ now fills his life. It is important to remember that we can be the instruments God wants to use to reach our families for Christ.

71

3. **As a true disciple of Jesus Christ, you will make personal sacrifices.**

Since the first century, true Christians have suffered much persecution because they faithfully followed and obeyed Jesus Christ. Is it possible that we are exempt just because we live in the 21st century? Of course not! Luke 14:27 declares, *whosoever doth not bear his _____, and come after me, cannot be my disciple.* When the "cross" is mentioned, it is not speaking of some sickness or difficulty, but a "personal sacrifice" of unconditional obedience to Jesus Christ. It is truly a sacrifice of our own personal desires for the purpose of following the will of Jesus Christ. In 2nd Timothy 3:12, the Apostle Paul declares with certainty, *Yea, and all that will live _____ [a life which God requires] in Christ Jesus shall suffer persecution.* The Apostle Peter reminds us in 1st Peter 1:6-9 that the Christian life is not easy with all its trials and afflictions: *Wherein ye greatly _____, though now for a season, if need be, ye are in heaviness through manifold temptations* [trials]. Jesus Christ affirmed in John 16:33, *These things I have spoken unto you, that in me ye might have peace. In the world ye shall have tribulation: but be of good cheer; I have overcome the world.* Yes! There will be personal sacrifices that we will make, but we do it with joy.

4. **As a true disciple of Jesus Christ, it is important to count the cost of being a Christian.**

In Luke 14:28-30, Jesus talks about the construction of a tower that was never completed. His asked the multitude, *For which of you, intending to build a tower, sitteth not down first, and counteth the cost, whether he have sufficient to finish it? Lest haply, after he hath laid the foundation, and is not able to _____ it, all that behold it begin to mock him, saying, This man began to build, and was not able to finish.* Jesus Christ uses this illustration to let us know that it is necessary to count the cost before we give ourselves to Him. You need to examine your heart, for it is a full commitment to God. Many who do not first consider the cost turn back and make a mockery of the Gospel. Consequently, they end up becoming the enemy of God. There are those that look at the true Christian and see that his life is peaceful, happy and confident.

They desire the same, so they made a "decision or profession of faith," but they were not sincere with God or with themselves. The Apostle Peter warns in 2nd Peter 2:20-22 of the danger of making a false decision: *For if after they have escaped the pollutions of the world through the knowledge of the Lord and Savior Jesus Christ, they are again entangled therein, and overcome, the latter end is worse with them than the beginning. For it had been better for them not to have known the way of righteousness, than, after they have known it, to _____ from the holy commandment delivered unto them. But it is happened unto them according to the true proverb, the dog is turned to his own vomit again; and the sow that was washed to her wallowing in the mire.* Also, in Luke 9:62, *Jesus said, unto him, No man, having put his hand to the plow, and looking _____, is fit for the kingdom of God.* The act of "having put his hand to the plow," refers to someone who has understood God's plan for salvation, repented of his sins and has given himself wholeheartedly to Jesus Christ. When someone is sincere with God and truly born again, nothing or no one can cause him to turn back. The Apostle Paul said in Hebrews 10:39, *But we are _____ of them who drawback unto perdition; but of them that believe to the saving of the soul.*

5. **As a true disciple of Jesus Christ, you will have battles against your enemy, Satan.**

In Luke 14:31-32, Jesus compares the Christian life with warfare: *Or what king, going to make war against another king, sitteth not down first, and consulteth whether he be able with ten thousand to meet him that cometh against him with twenty thousand? Or else, while the other is yet a great way off, he sendeth an ambassage* [ambassador], *and desireth conditions of _____.* The Apostle Paul warns us of dangers and reminds us that we must receive help from God in order to be victorious in our battles against Satan. He gives all Christians an important order in Ephesians 6:11-12: *Put on the whole _____ of God, that ye may be able to stand against the wiles of the devil. For we wrestle not against flesh and blood, but against principalities, against powers, against the rulers of the darkness of this world, against spiritual wickedness in high places.* If you are under the conviction of the Holy Spirit, but think that the Christian life will be too hard, you should permit God to help you overcome that fear. First, you must decide whether God can do what He promises in His Word. Romans 8:31 says, *What shall we then say to these things? If God be for us, _____ can be against us?* If you do not want to trust in Jesus Christ as your great Protector and Helper, Luke 14:32 suggests that a message be sent to the enemy, Satan, asking him for "conditions of peace." There is absolutely nothing that you have to do, because Satan already is in control of your life. Jesus Christ wants you to know that the Christian life is one battle after another. **God wants you to completely trust Him.**

6. **As a true disciple of Jesus Christ, He commands you to forsake all that you have.**

In Luke 14:33 Jesus Christ declares, *So likewise, whosoever he be of you that **forsaketh** not _____ that he hath, he cannot be my disciple.* Many stumble over this passage thinking that it is commanding us to forsake all our earthly possessions. We have to recognize that we cannot trust in our possessions in order to acquire salvation or favor with God. Jesus Christ spoke to the rich young ruler declaring almost the same thing in Mark 10:17-23: *And when he was gone forth into the way, there came one running, and kneeled to him, and asked him, Good Master, what shall I do that I may inherit eternal life? And Jesus said unto him, Why callest thou me good? There is none good but one, that is, God. Thou knowest the commandments, Do not commit adultery, Do not kill, Do not steal, Do not bear false witness, Defraud not, Honour thy father and mother. And he answered and said unto him, Master, all these have I observed from my youth. Then Jesus beholding him loved him, and said unto him, One thing thou lackest: go thy way, _____ whatsoever thou hast, and _____ to the poor, and thou shalt have treasure in Heaven: and come, take up the cross, and follow me. And he was sad at that saying, and went away grieved: for he had great possessions. And Jesus looked round about, and saith unto his disciples, How hardly shall they that have riches enter into the kingdom of God!* Why was Jesus so drastic with him? Mark 10:24 gives the reason – Jesus Christ knew the heart of this young man and said, *how hard is it for them that _____ in riches to enter into the kingdom of God!* This young man had placed his trust in what he thought he could do to achieve his entrance into Heaven. He loved his possessions more than God. God knows our intentions and sees our heart. In Mark 10:26-27, the apostles were astonished at Jesus' response and asked, *Who then can be saved? And Jesus looking upon them saith, with men it is _____, but not with God: for with God all things are possible.* Salvation only comes through the work of God!

The desire of the Apostle Paul was to obey the Lord Jesus Christ in everything he did. We read his testimony in Philippians 3:7-8. Notice his attitude in verse 8: *Yea doubtless, and I count all things but _____ for the excellency of the knowledge of Christ Jesus my Lord: for whom I have suffered the loss of all things, and do count them but dung, that I may win* [please] *Christ.* Neither the Apostle Paul, nor anyone else can obtain salvation by what he can give or do! God faithfully provided all of Paul's needs as described in Philippians 4:12: *I know both how to be abased* [humiliated or have need], *and I know how to abound: everywhere and in all things I am instructed both to be full and to be hungry, both to abound and to suffer need.* The Apostle Paul had given himself totally to the Lord to be used as God desired. He had his heart open to God so that he could do His will. All that he had and did was for the honor and glory of Jesus Christ.

7. **As a true disciple of Jesus Christ, you must be genuine and not just an imitation.**

The last teaching that Jesus Christ mentioned in Luke 14:34 is regarding salt: *Salt is good: but if the salt have _____ his savour, wherewith shall it be seasoned?* Some substances can appear to be salt, but if it does not have the qualities of true salt, what good is it? True salt never losses its properties of sodium chloride. Luke 14:35 declares, *It is neither fit for the land, nor yet for the dunghill.* God wants us to be a genuine Christian and not just to appear as one. Many say they are Christians, when they really are not. So Christ warns us about those that just make a "profession of faith." What good is this profession? He finishes this passage by saying, *He that hath ears to hear, let him hear.* It is crucial for us to be true and authentic Christians. So many people put on a good act and talk like a Christian, but remember, God knows the difference!

REVIEW QUESTIONS – CHAPTER 5

SALVATION: THE SPIRITUAL BIRTH

1. Do you realize that you are a terrible sinner? _____

2. Why is salvation necessary? _____
   _____

3. How did God show His love? (Romans 5:8) _____
   _____
   _____

4. How can you receive salvation? (Mark 1:15; Ephesians 2:8-9) _____
   _____
   _____

5. Is repentance for our sinful condition necessary for salvation? _____
   Why? _____
   _____

6. Is it possible to repent of your sins, place our complete faith in Jesus Christ with all your heart, and then keep it a secret? _____

7. When you become a true Christian, is it possible that you will suffer persecution from your family and friends because of your new life in Jesus Christ? _____

8. Do you believe with all your heart that Jesus Christ died on the cross and arose from the dead, completely paying the debt for your sin? _____

9. Are you truly repentant of all your known sins, recognizing they are offenses against God? _____

10. Do you want God's will to be done in your life? _____ Are you ready to give yourself wholeheartedly to the Lord Jesus Christ and to become His property? _____

Do you understand the preceding lessons? _____ If you have any doubts, you should study again the preceding chapters and talk with your counselor about your doubts.

Read the following very carefully, for this is not a decision to make carelessly.

Are you repentant for all your sins? _____ Are you ready to give yourself to Jesus Christ, trusting in Him with all your heart? _____ If it is your desire, at this moment you can give yourself to Jesus Christ.

With all sincerity, pray to God with true faith acknowledging that the Lord Jesus Christ died on the cross to pay the debt for your sin, and physically arose from the dead to save you. Recognize your terrible, sinful condition and truly express repentance for your sin. As you pour out your heart to Him, ask for forgiveness for your sin. Believing in the Lord Jesus Christ as your personal Savior, ask Him to save you. Give yourself to Jesus Christ, recognizing His authority over your life forever.

You can pray on your knees, standing or sitting. The position of the body is not important, but the condition of your heart is very important. **I trust that you will give yourself to Jesus Christ today.** *Please close the book, close your eyes in reverence to God and pour out your heart to Him. Please pray aloud so that you will not be distracted.*

Did you give yourself completely to the Lord Jesus Christ, recognizing Him as your only sufficient Savior?____ Did you repent of your sin and truly give yourself to Jesus Christ with all your heart? _____ Do you belong to Him? _____ Do you know for sure you are saved? _____ Are you saved for all eternity or can you lose your salvation? _____
_____ Your assurance of salvation is not based upon an emotional feeling, but on the Word of God. Please study the following passages and choose one verse that clearly gives you assurance of salvation: John 10:28-29; Ephesians 2:1-5; 2nd Timothy 1:12; Romans 8:16; 1st John 5:10-15; and Hebrews 7:25.

Please write the full verse that you have selected here. _____
_____
_____
_____

If you have truly been converted to our Lord Jesus Christ, you should remember this important date when you were born-again and became a child of God.

_____   _____
Your signature   Date

Now that you belong to Jesus Christ you have the following responsibilities:

1. You need to read the Bible every day to be able to grow spiritually. (Psalm 119:105; 1st Peter 2:2; Joshua 1:8)

2. Take time to pray every day, for God always desires to have intimate fellowship with His children. (Hebrews 4:15-16; 1st Timothy 2:1-3) You should always give thanks to God and to Jesus Christ for your salvation. You can tell Him in prayer right now.

3. Attend all the services and Bible studies in a Fundamental Bible-believing church where the sound doctrine of the Word of God is truly preached so that you can receive teaching and correction to help you grow spiritually in your new life in Jesus Christ. (Hebrews 10:25; 2nd Peter 3:18)

4. You need to be baptized in water to identify yourself publicly with Jesus Christ and the local church where you are faithfully attending. (Acts 2:41-47; Matthew 28:19)

5. You have the privilege to witness to others regarding your new life and faith in the Lord Jesus Christ, for your friends need to hear the reason for your changed life. (Mark 16:15; Romans 1:16; 1st Thessalonians 1:9-10)

God has forgiven you and has received you into His family from the moment that you gave yourself to Jesus Christ. The Holy Spirit has come into your life to guide you. He has given you peace and joy that the world cannot give. You need to tell others of your conversion. God places a great responsibility on us to share our testimony with others regarding our salvation so that they can also hear and believe. May God richly bless you!

If it is possible please write and share the news of your conversion with me: philippi@becoming-a-christian.org

If you do not attend a church that is faithfully teaching the Word of God, we will try to recommend a church in your area where you can receive the teaching of sound doctrine. Please contact me at the following address:

Pastor Myron L. Philippi
Becoming a Christian Org. Inc.
6465 99th Way N. #17B
St. Petersburg, FL 33708
727-393-7846
philippi@becoming-a-christian.org

The assurance of salvation does not come from yourself, from good feelings, or from your personal ideas, but from the Bible. Please study the next lesson to understand more about the assurance of salvation for the true believer.

Chapter Six

The Security of the True Christian

My sheep hear my voice, and I know them, and they follow me:
and I give unto them eternal life; and they shall never perish,
neither shall any man pluck them out of my hand.
My Father, which gave them me, is greater than all;
and no man is able to pluck them out of my Father's hand.

John 10:27-29

YES, WE CAN KNOW THAT WE ARE SAVED!

The Apostle Paul was transformed by Jesus Christ, and now he gives a strong testimony of the great security of his salvation in 2nd Timothy 1:12: *For the which cause I also suffer these things: nevertheless I am not ashamed: for I _____ whom I have believed, and am persuaded that he is able to keep that which I have committed unto him against that day.* God wants us to know with complete assurance that we are saved and that we belong to Jesus Christ even when things seem to go terribly wrong. To whom do you belong? _____ Hebrews 12:2 assures us that Jesus Christ is *the _____ and finisher of our faith; who for the joy that was set before him endured the cross, despising the shame, and is set down at the right hand of the throne of God.* Furthermore, Jesus Christ is the only Mediator between God the Father and us, providing His complete forgiveness. (1st Timothy 2:5-6) Because God has forgiven us, the guilt of sin has been removed making it possible for man to be reconciled to God and be in harmony with Him. This transpired when Jesus Christ our Savior made a covenant with the human race, dying on the cross. However, the only way this covenant can be effective is when the sinner repents of his sin and gives himself to Jesus Christ. With complete clarity, the Bible teaches that the true believer can have the assurance of salvation and eternal life, which comes only through the Word of God.

I. THE ASSURANCE OF GOD'S FORGIVENESS

The Bible teaches us that true salvation comes directly from God. It is only through the death, burial, and resurrection of Jesus Christ that we have the means provided by God for our eternal salvation. We cannot add anything to what the Lord Jesus Christ did for us in His perfect sacrifice by shedding His blood, and dying on the cross for us; however, without His resurrection there would be no salvation. We reap the benefits of this provision when we repent of our sins, trust Christ as our Savior and give ourselves to Him with our whole heart.

1. The provision of forgiveness through Jesus Christ

    a. Jesus Christ gave His life and shed His blood on the cross for us. Ephesians 1:5-7 declares, *Having predestinated us unto the adoption of children by Jesus Christ to himself, according to the good pleasure of his will, to the praise of the glory of his grace, wherein He hath made us accepted in the Beloved. In whom we have _____ through His blood, the forgiveness of sins, according to the riches of His grace.*

    b. God gave His specific conditions in His Word enabling us to receive His forgiveness. The Word of God tells us if we confess our sins with true repentance there will be immediate pardon from God and fellowship will be reestablished with Him. We should not endeavor to defend our sinful actions. King David tried to hide his sin, but later the Prophet Nathan confronted him with God's Word. His conscience convicted him of his terrible sin and he humbly confessed it to God. Psalm 32:5 shows his true attitude: *I acknowledged my sin unto thee, and mine iniquity have I not hid. I said, I will _____ my transgressions unto the Lord;*

and thou forgavest the iniquity of my sin. It is very important that we maintain our life transparent and not try to hide our sins.

Proverbs 28:13 says, *He that covereth his sins shall not prosper: but whoso _____ and _____ them shall have mercy.* Jesus Christ is our Lawyer to defend us before God. This truth is taught in 1ˢᵗ John 2:1: *And if any _____ sin, we have a advocate* [Lawyer or go-between] *with the Father, Jesus Christ the righteous.* Our faithful and just Lawyer, Jesus Christ, knows our problems and how to present our case before God, our Judge. He intercedes for us and we are forgiven (pardoned). Immediately, our communication and fellowship is reestablished with our Father. God always desires to have intimate fellowship with His children.

2. The promise of forgiveness by God

   a. God promises that He will show mercy to us if we are sincere when asking Him for forgiveness for our sins. Isaiah 55:7 gives the command: *Let the wicked forsake his way, and the unrighteous man his thoughts: and let him return unto the Lord, and He will have _____ upon him; and to our God, for He will abundantly pardon.* If we truly repent and confess our sins to Christ, He assures us of His forgives as 1ˢᵗ John 1:9 declares: *He is faithful and just to _____ us our sins, and to cleanse us from all unrighteousness.* The word, *confess* means – "to say the same thing or be in agreement with." In this case God wants us to recognize what we have done wrong and agree with Him. It is not just to admit that we have done wrong, but truly be repentant for our sins, recognizing that we have offended God and then forsake them to receive His mercy. Therefore, we have to confess our sin, name them, and with repentance ask Jesus Christ for forgiveness. He does forgive us and cleanses us from all sin. This confession is done by means of direct prayer to God as soon as we realize that we have sinned.

   b. Upon asking for forgiveness, what does God promise to do with our sin? Psalm 103:12 states, *As far as the east is from the west, so far hath he _____ our transgressions from us.* Micah 7:19 also assures us, *He will turn again, he will have compassion upon us; he will subdue our iniquities; and thou wilt _____ all their sins into the depths of the sea.* In

81

Hebrews 10:17 Jesus Christ promised, *And their _____ and iniquities will I remember no more.* Psalm 32:1-2 affirms, *Blessed is he whose transgression is forgiven, whose _____ is covered. Blessed is the man unto whom the Lord imputeth not iniquity, and in whose spirit there is no guile.*

3. The results of confessing our sins to God

    a. God hears us when we recognize our sins, humble ourselves and confess them to Him. 2nd Chronicles 7:14-15 affirms, *If my people, which are called by my name, shall _____ themselves, and pray, and seek my face, and turn from their wicked ways; then will I hear from Heaven, and **will forgive their sin**, and will heal their land. Now mine eyes shall be open, and mine ears attent unto the prayer that is made in this place.* God acts in love and tenderness toward us, desiring the best for us, but we must be sincere and repent of our sinful ways.

    b. Because we are members of God's family, the blood of Jesus Christ is applied to each one of us, and is sufficient to cleanse us from all our sins – past, present, and even those of the future. The Apostle John encourages us in 1st John 1:7 to maintain true fellowship with Christ: *But if we walk in the light, as he is in the light, we have _____ one with another, and the blood of Jesus Christ his Son cleanseth us from all sin.*

    c. God gives us joy and peace. Romans 15:13 declares, *Now the God of hope fill you with all joy and peace in believing, that ye may _____ in hope, through the power of the Holy Ghost.* After confessing our sins, we have to avoid those things that Satan wants to use to tempt us. In 2nd Timothy 2:22, the Apostle Paul warns Timothy: *Flee also youthful lusts: but _____ righteousness, faith, charity* [love], *peace, with them that call on the Lord out of a pure heart.* By doing this, He can bless us with His peace and joy.

4. The results of unconfessed sin

    a. Sin cannot make you lose your salvation, but sin will separate you from fellowship with God, just like disobedience disrupts your fellowship with your natural parents. If you refuse to recognize and confess your sins, you cannot enjoy the same relationship with God as previously experienced. Is it possible that God can have fellowship with you and overlook your sins? _____ How can you reestablish your fellowship with God? The Apostle Paul instructs us in 2nd Corinthians 7:1, *Having therefore these promises, dearly beloved, let us _____ ourselves from all filthiness of the flesh and spirit, perfecting holiness in the fear of God.* With God's help we must remove sinful and careless practices from our life.

b. Sin is always an offence against the very nature of God. As a result, we can expect God's discipline, not His blessings. If we continue in our sin, we can expect that our Father, who loves us so much, will discipline us like any father disciplines a disobedient son. True love is manifested in discipline. Hebrews 12:5-11 assures us that the purpose of discipline is to bring us to obedience: *My son, despise not thou the chastening of the Lord, nor faint when thou art _____ of him: for whom the Lord loveth he chasteneth, and scourgeth every son whom he receiveth. If ye endure chastening, God dealeth with you as with sons; for what son is he whom the father chasteneth not? . . . Now no chastening for the present seemeth to be joyous, but grievous: nevertheless afterward it yieldeth the peaceable fruit of righteousness unto them which are exercised* [trained] *thereby.* God wants us to hate sin as He hates sin, and He wants us to judge sin as He judges sin. We have to act drastically with our own sin and judge it.

The Apostle Paul gives the warning in 2nd Corinthians 5:10, that one day we will give account to God for what we have done: *For we must all appear before the judgment seat of Christ; that every one may receive the things done in his body, according to that he hath done, whether it be _____ or _____.* This not only teaches that we will receive rewards at the Judgment Seat of Christ, but it also teaches that we will give an account of ourselves for willful, unconfessed sin. We have to give an account of ourselves for our actions to our All-knowing (Omniscient) God. If sins have not been confessed, is it possible for the true Christian to be condemned to the Lake of Fire? **No!** According to Romans 8:1, *There is therefore now _____ condemnation to them which are in Christ Jesus, who walk not after the flesh, but after the Spirit.*

c. Those who claims to be saved, but love and practice sin are not truly of God. They are not saved! This is taught in the original language of the New Testament. The following verses refer to those who "practice sin." It declares in 1st John 3:6-9, *Whosoever abideth in him sinneth not* [does not practice sin]: *whosoever sinneth* [practices sin] *hath not seen him, neither known him. Little children, let no man deceive you: he that doeth righteousness is righteous, even as he is* _____. *He that committeth sin* [practices sin] *is of the devil; for the devil sinneth from the beginning. For this purpose the Son of God was manifested, that he might destroy the works of the devil. Whosoever is born of God doth not commit sin* [practice sin]*; for His seed* [His Spirit] *remaineth in him: and he cannot sin* [practice sin]*, because he is born of God.*

d. What does God say regarding the person who has the concept that he has never sinned? It declares in 1st John 1:8, *If we say that we have no sin, we* _____ *ourselves, and the truth is not in us.* We should not deny that we have sinned, but recognize immediately what we have done and confess it. Again this truth is repeated in 1st John 1:10: *If we say that we have not sinned, we make him a* _____, *and his Word is not in us.* Those who deny the fact that they are sinners are actually calling God a liar and do not belong to God. Is it possible for God to lie? **NEVER!**

II. THE ASSURANCE OF SALVATION

You should not permit Satan to rob you of your security if you really belong to Jesus Christ. On the other hand, there are many who believe they are in the truth, when in reality they are in error. This is the worst type of deception one can experience. You should not permit your thoughts to betray you, believing that you are saved, if in reality you are lost. Salvation is based upon the grace of God, which brings us to faith and confidence in Christ. You cannot depend upon your feelings and emotions for the security of your salvation.

1. We can have the assurance of our salvation because of what God the Father has done.

a. True salvation comes from God. The Bible teaches us that the security of true salvation comes from God and not of ourselves. 1st Peter 2:9-10 says, *But ye are a chosen generation, a royal priesthood, an holy nation, a peculiar* [acquired] *people; that ye should shew forth the praises of him who hath called you out of*

_____ *into his marvelous light; which in time past were not a people, but are now the people of God: which had not obtained mercy, but now have obtained mercy.* The Apostle Paul confirms this in Philippians 3:20: *For our conversation* [citizenship] *is in Heaven; from whence also we look for the Savior, the Lord Jesus Christ.* The plan of salvation began and ended with God. It is His plan and He fulfilled it in order to save us. When a person repents of his sin, puts his faith in the Lord Jesus Christ, and gives himself to Him, God makes him His son. In the same way that I will always be the son of my parents, even so my relationship of being a son of God will be forever. Because I was born into the family of God, I can never lose this relationship.

b. God gave us His righteousness. The Apostle Paul, in Romans 4:1-5, tells us how we **"receive" Jesus Christ**. Verse 3 asks a question to make us think: *For what saith the Scripture? Abraham* _____ *God, and it was **counted** unto him for righteousness.* The word, **counted** is a term used in accounting as an action that occurs when a transfer is made from one account to another. This transfer was made from God's account to Abraham's account. In other words, when Abraham trusted Christ as his substitute and personal Savior he **"received"** salvation. Salvation was placed to his account, because by faith he was adopted into the family of God. God deposits this same salvation to our account only when we repent of our sin and give ourselves to the Lord Jesus Christ, trusting in Him as our personal Savior. Have you **"received"** this salvation to your account? _____ Christ declared in John 1:12, *But as many as **received** him, to them gave he power* [authority] *to become the sons of God, even to them that* _____ *on his name.* **This action of "receiving" is the result of depositing our full confidence in Jesus Christ and He comes into our life to live in us forever.**

c. We are His for all eternity. The true Christian is safe in the hands of God. Many falsely teach that the believer can lose the salvation that God has given to him. The Lord Jesus Christ affirms in John 10:27, *My sheep hear my voice, and I know* _____, *and **they follow me**.* If you are truly saved, you are one of His sheep, **you will hear His Word and you will faithfully follow Him.** John 10:28-29 confirms that the salvation that Jesus Christ gives us is eternal: *And I give unto them eternal life; and they shall _____ perish, neither shall any man pluck them out of my hand. My Father, which gave them me, is greater than all; and no man is able to pluck them out of my Father's hand.* **We are saved for all eternity!** We have read various passages that give the true Christian the assurance of his salvation. I strongly urge you to memorize some of the Bible passages that you have studied regarding the assurance of salvation.

2. We can have the assurance of our salvation because of what God the Son has done.

    a. Philippians 2:6-8 briefly highlights the ministry and work of the Lord Jesus Christ: *Who, being in the form of God, thought it not robbery to be equal with God: but made himself of no reputation, and took upon him the form of a servant, and was made in the likeness of men: and being found in fashion as a man, he humbled himself, and became _____ unto death, even the death of the cross.* This complete plan of salvation was given by God and taught throughout the Bible as revealed in Ephesians 1:5-7: *Having predestinated us unto the adoption of children by Jesus Christ to himself, according to the good pleasure of his will, to the praise of the glory of his grace, wherein he hath made us accepted in the beloved. In whom _____ have redemption through his blood, the forgiveness of_____, according to the riches of his grace.*

    b. From the time that sin entered into the world, God required a blood sacrifice as a symbol or shadow of that which was to come. It was necessary that Jesus Christ be crucified in order to fulfill all the Old Testament prophecies regarding the shedding of the blood of God's special sacrifice. Hebrews 9:22 explains, *And almost all things are by the law purged with blood; and without shedding of _____ is no remission* (no forgiveness). Jesus Christ is the fulfillment of all those sacrifices. Our salvation was paid for as the wrath of God was poured out upon Jesus Christ on the cross. After three days in the tomb, Jesus Christ **physically arose** to assure us that He had done all that was necessary to provide eternal salvation for us. There is nothing more for God to do in order to save us. We can only receive salvation through faith, being repentant for our sin and giving ourselves to the Lord Jesus Christ. 1st Peter 3:18 gives a concise explanation of why Jesus had to die: *For Christ also hath _____ suffered for sins, the just for the unjust,* **that he might bring us to God**, *being put to death in the flesh, but quickened* [alive] *by the Spirit.* (By saying, "quickened" tells us that the spirit never dies.)

c. Time after time the Bible reminds us that Jesus Christ finished His work so that it would never have to be repeated, nor continued in a religious ceremony as some practice. Unfortunately, there are religious people who try to achieve forgiveness by means of religious rites and traditions, which God rejects. Hebrews 10:11 declares, *Every priest standeth daily ministering and offering oftentimes the same sacrifices, which can _____ take away sins.* Hebrews 10:12 explains that only one sacrifice is valid: *But this man* [Jesus Christ], *after he had offered _____* **sacrifice** *for sins* **forever**, *sat down on the right hand of God.* When reading Hebrews 9:12 and 25-28, you will clearly understand that the ceremony of the "Sacrifice of the Mass" is anti-biblical. Again, Hebrews 10:10 and 14 confirms this teaching, *By the which will we are sanctified through the offering of the body of Jesus Christ* **once for all** *. . . For by one offering he hath perfected forever them that are sanctified.* Throughout the Bible the term **sanctified** is used, which means – "separated for the use of God."

3. We can have the assurance of our salvation because of what God the Holy Spirit has done.

a. When we gave ourselves to the Lord Jesus Christ we were immediately "baptized" into the family of God by the Holy Spirit. 1ˢᵗ Corinthians 12:13 says, *For by one Spirit are we all _____ into one body.* The word, **baptism** means – "placed into." In other words, we have been "placed into" the family of God. All who have placed their confidence in Jesus Christ as their Savior have been placed into the body of Christ, which is His Church. The baptism of the Holy Spirit is the act of placing the true believer into the family of God. This is shown in Ephesians 4:4-6: *There is one body, and one Spirit, even as ye are called in one hope of your calling; One Lord, one faith, _____* **baptism**, *One God and Father of all, who is above all, and through all, and in you all.* This baptism is not in water, but is **the placement of the true Christian into the family of God forever**. This baptism of the Holy Spirit can only happen one time.

b. When we gave ourselves to Jesus Christ, the Holy Spirit entered our life and put upon us His **seal of ownership**. The Apostle Paul confirms this in 2nd Corinthians 3:3-4: *Forasmuch as ye are manifestly declared to be the epistle of Christ ministered by us, written not with ink, but with the Spirit of the living God; not in tables of stone, but in fleshy tables of the _____. And such trust have we through Christ to God-ward.* When were we sealed by the Holy Spirit? Ephesians 1:13 gives the answer: *In whom ye also trusted, after that ye heard the word of truth, the Gospel of your salvation: in whom also after that ye _____, ye were sealed with that Holy Spirit of promise.* Why is it important that God put His seal upon us? The explanation is given in Ephesians 1:14: *Which is the earnest* [the assurance or down payment] *of our inheritance until the redemption of the purchased possession, unto the praise of His glory.* If we make a contract to purchase a property, a deed is made. Both the buyer and the seller sign it and an official seal is placed on it. From that moment the new owner has the **assurance** that the property belongs to him. We, who are the property of Jesus Christ, have the seal of the Holy Spirit upon our life forever. Philippians 1:6 assures us that God will finish the work that He started: *Being **confident** of this very thing, that he which hath _____ a good work in you will perform it until the day of Jesus Christ.* **We are His property forever!**

c. The Holy Spirit lives in every Christian from the moment that he trusts in Jesus Christ as his Savior. We do not receive our salvation first and the Holy Spirit afterwards. The Holy Spirit does not come into us little by little. Jesus Christ taught a great truth, in John 3:34, that we should never forget: *For God giveth **not** the Spirit by _____ unto him.* Jesus declares in John 14:17, *Even the Spirit of truth; whom the world cannot receive, because it seeth him not, neither knoweth him: but ye know him; for he _____ with you, and shall be in you.* If you have put your trust in Jesus Christ as your Savior, the Holy Spirit lives in you! What should we think about Christians who sin? Can they lose their salvation? In the light of God's Word, **the true Christian does not lose his salvation** because he has sinned; however, the Holy Spirit will bring conviction, repentance and the confession of his sin to God. In contrast, when a person has not given himself to Jesus Christ, his sin will not disturb him, and he will continue in his sin. This shows that he does not have the Holy Spirit as declared in Romans 8:9: *if any man have _____ the Spirit of Christ, he is _____ of His.*

4. We can have the assurance of our salvation because of what the Bible promises.

   a. 1st John 5:10 teaches, *He that believeth* [deposits his trust] *on the Son of God hath the _____ in himself.* The **witness**, is the Spirit of God, who came to dwell in us when we gave ourselves to Jesus Christ! Romans 8:16 explains, *The Spirit itself beareth witness with our spirit, that we are the children of God.* The true Christian knows in his heart that he is a son of God. In 1st John 5:11-13 the Apostle John declared, *And this is the record, that God hath given to us eternal life, and this life is in his Son. He that hath the Son hath life; and he that hath not the Son of God hath not life. These things have I written unto you that believe* [those who have deposited their confidence] *on the **name** of the Son of God; that ye may _____ that ye have eternal life, and that ye may believe on the **name** of the Son of God.* The word, **name** refers to everything that the name of the Son of God represents, because of who He is, and what He did when he died and arose from the dead to save us. God wants us to know that we belong to Him. Are you sure that you are saved and truly a son of God? _____

   b. The Bible is full of promises of assurance of salvation for the true Christian. John 5:24 gives us another confirmation of our salvation: *He that heareth my word, and believeth on Him that sent me, hath _____ life, and shall not come into condemnation; but is passed from death unto life.*

   c. God guides His children. Romans 8:14 declares, *For as many as are led by the Spirit of God, they are the _____ of God.* We should desire to be continually led by God through the teaching of His Word; therefore, we should be faithful in the study of God's Word.

   d. Even though the Apostle Paul was receiving much persecution, with a great assurance of his salvation, he gave this testimony in 2nd Timothy 1:12: *For the which cause I also suffer these things: nevertheless I am not ashamed: for I _____ whom I have believed, and am persuaded that he is able to keep that which I have committed unto him against that day.* This testimony also should be yours! God wants you to **know for sure that you are saved.** This is an important verse to memorize and share with others.

III. THE RESULTS OF SALVATION

When a person has given himself by faith to Christ, God produces many changes in his life and gives this assurance to the believer.

1. We have **a new birth** as a result of our salvation.

    Christ Jesus declared in John 3:3, *Verily, verily, I say unto thee, except a man be _____ again, he cannot see the kingdom of God.* God's Word confirms this spiritual birth in 1ˢᵗ Peter 1:23: *Being _____ again, not of corruptible seed, but of incorruptible, by the word of God, which liveth and abideth forever.* How is this change accomplished? It is explained in Ezekiel 36:26-27: *A new _____ also will I give you, and a new _____ will I put within you: and I will take away the stony heart out of your flesh, and I will give you a heart of flesh. And I will put my _____ within you, and cause you to walk in my statutes, and ye shall keep my judgments, and do them.* What a blessing!

2. We have **a new life** as a result of our salvation.

    In 1ˢᵗ John 5:12-13 the Apostle John gives assurance to the new believer: *And this is the record, that God hath given to us eternal life, and this _____ is in his Son. He that hath the Son hath life; and he that hath not the Son of God hath not life. These things have I written unto you that believe* [to deposit our complete confidence] *on the name of the Son of God; that ye may know that ye have eternal _____, and that ye may believe* [believe more and more] *on the name of the Son of God.* In 2ⁿᵈ Corinthians 5:17, the Apostle Paul gives three biblical truths that sum up the changes in the life of the believer: *Therefore if any man be in Christ, he is a _____ creature: _____ things are passed away; behold, all things are become _____.* Jesus Christ transforms the life of those who have placed their confidence in Him. 2ⁿᵈ Corinthians 5:18 confirms the origin of this work: *all things are of God, who hath reconciled us to himself by Jesus Christ, and hath given to us the ministry of reconciliation.* Only God can do this in your life. 1ˢᵗ Peter 2:2 instructs those who are born again: *As newborn babes, desire the sincere* _____ *of the Word, that ye may grow thereby.* What happens if someone does not want to receive this spiritual food? It is sad, because it shows that he does not love God, nor is there a desire to have fellowship with Him. Consequently, he does not show evidence of the working of the Holy Spirit in his life. There is no evidence of a new life.

3.   We have **a new family** as a result of our salvation.

In Jesus Christ we became part of a new family. Now I can exclaim, "I am one of God's children and I know that I belong to Him!" John 1:12 says, *But as many as received him, to them gave he power* [authority] *to become the sons of God, even to them that believe* [completely trust] *on his name.* God has made us members of His family! God is our Father and all true believers are our new brothers and sisters. This is confirmed in Hebrews 2:11, *For both He that sanctifieth* [Christ Jesus] *and they who are sanctified* [the true believers] *are all of one: for which cause he is not ashamed to call them* _____. Ephesians 2:19 also confirms this relationship: *Now therefore ye are no more strangers and foreigners, but fellowcitizens with the saints, and of the* _____ *of God.* Truly, we are of the family of God! The Apostle exclaims in 1st John 3:1-2, *Behold, what manner of love the Father hath bestowed upon us, that we should be called the* _____ *of God: therefore the world knoweth us not, because it knew him not. Beloved, now are we the sons of God. . .*

4.   We have **a new relationship** as a result of our salvation.

a.   We are God's **friends!** When we trust in Christ as our personal Savior, God gives us a new relationship. Jesus Christ expressed this relationship in John 15:14-15: *Ye are my friends, if ye do whatsoever I command you. Henceforth I call you not servants; for the servant knoweth not what his lord doeth: but I have called you* _____; *for all things that I have heard of my Father I have made known unto you.* Are you a friend of God? _____ How do you show it? _____
_____ Colossians 1:21-22 reminds us of our lost condition before we belonged to Jesus Christ: *And you, that were sometime alienated and enemies in your mind by wicked works, yet now hath he* _____ *in the body of his flesh through death, to present you holy and*

unblameable and unreproveable in his sight. What were the two conditions in the past that show that we were separated from God? 1. _____ 2. _____ Before we lived in disobedience to God, but when we trusted Jesus Christ as our Savior we became friends. James 2:23 tells about Abraham when he fully trusted God: *And the scripture was fulfilled which saith, Abraham believed God, and it was imputed unto him for righteousness: and he was called **the Friend of God.*** Now, we have the presence of Jesus Christ in our life and we are God's friends!

b. We are His **adopted sons** and therefore heirs of God. There are many passages of Scripture, which reveal our important relationship in the family of God. In 2nd Corinthians 6:18, the Apostle Paul quotes what God said in the Old Testament: *And will be a Father unto you, and ye shall be my _____ and daughters, saith the Lord Almighty.* Romans 8:15-17 declares, *For ye have not received the spirit of bondage again to fear; but ye have received the Spirit of adoption, whereby we cry, Abba, Father. The Spirit himself beareth witness with our spirit, that we are the _____ of God: And if children, then heirs; heirs of God, and joint-heirs with Christ; if so be that we suffer with him, that we may be also glorified together.*

c. We are **servants** of Jesus Christ. The Apostle Paul considered it a great privilege to be a servant of Jesus Christ and of all the brethren. He declared it repeatedly throughout his writings. In 2nd Corinthians 4:5 he mentioned, *For we preach not ourselves, but Christ Jesus the Lord; and ourselves your _____ for Jesus' sake.* We have an example in 1st Thessalonians 1:9 of how the brethren served the Lord: *For they themselves shew of us what manner of entering in we had unto you, and how ye turned to God from idols to _____ the living and true God.*

5. We have **a new name** as a result of our salvation.

In 1st Peter 1:15-16 we are admonished: *But as he which hath called you is holy, so be ye _____ in all manner of conversation* [manner of living]*: Be ye _____; for I am holy.* He has made us **saints**! Maybe you have never considered yourself to be a saint. It is possible that you have a wrong concept regarding the meaning of the word saint. The word *saint* means – "separated." The general biblical use of the word *saint* is, "separated from the world for the use of God." Jesus Christ has declared us "righteous" before God and has made us **saints**. In Colossians 1:22 we see the purpose of this sanctifying work of Jesus Christ: *to present you _____ and unblameable and unreproveable in His sight.* Every true Christian should see changes made by God in his life. Notice how the Apostle Paul uses the words "sanctified" and "saints" in his introduction to 1st Corinthians chapter 1 and verse 2: *Unto the church of God which is at Corinth, to them that are **sanctified** in Christ Jesus, called to be **saints**, with all that in every place call upon the name of Jesus Christ our Lord, both theirs and ours.* God wants us to remember that we belong to Him, and that we are to serve Him. As saints, we have been separated from the world for the use of Jesus Christ. When some religious people "pray to God through images," they refer to those images as "saints." We must understand that the Bible rejects the error of praying or attributing power to anyone or anything, but to God. The Bible strictly teaches against this practice!

6. We have **new responsibilities** as a result of our salvation.

   a. It is important that we live in fellowship with Jesus Christ. He desires that we live to please Him in all that we do. 1st John 1:7 talks about this fellowship: *But if we walk in the light, as he is in the light, we have _____ one with another.* Since it is impossible to live without sinning, God has made a provision for us. Even though we live in the 21st century, God has made a provision to forgive our sin because of what He did for us when He died on the cross to save us. This verse continues by stating: *and the blood of Jesus Christ his Son cleanseth us from all sin.* We are told how to receive this forgiveness in 1st John 1:9: *If we confess our sins* [to Christ Jesus], *he is faithful and just to _____ us our sins, and to cleanse us from all unrighteousness.*

   b. After saving us, God wants to see action on our part. He tells us to clean up the things in our life that are in direct opposition to our new God-given nature. In 2nd Corinthians 7:1, the Apostle Paul pleads with all believers: *Having therefore these promises, dearly beloved, let us _____ ourselves from all filthiness of the flesh and spirit, perfecting holiness in the fear of God.* God does not give us any options. It is extremely important to maintain our life transparent and not hold on to sin. We should never hide our sin, but confess it to Jesus Christ. Proverbs 28:13 gives us a warning and a promise: *He that covereth his sins shall not prosper: but whoso confesseth and forsaketh them shall have _____.*

7. We have a **new love** as a result of our salvation.

   a. There are no limits to our love, because God has given us His love! Romans 5:5 helps us to understand that *the _____ of God is shed abroad in our hearts by the Holy Ghost which is given unto us.* God always shows His love to us. His love has no limits. One of the most convincing evidences that a person is saved is the love of God manifested in his life day by day. When Christ has changed our heart, He also wants to transform our thoughts and actions. The former hostility that we had is replaced by His holy love. In Mark 12:30-31, Jesus Christ reminded them of the first and great commandment: *And thou shalt love the Lord thy God with all thy heart, and with all thy _____, and with all thy _____, and with all thy _____: this is the first commandment. And the second is like, namely this, Thou shalt love thy neighbor as thyself.* An intense love for God and a pure love for others now exist in the deepest sentiments of the regenerated life!

   b. The Apostle John could talk with authority, because he repeated the Words of Christ when he said in John 13:34: *A new commandment I give unto you, that ye love one another; as I have _____ you, that ye also love one another.* **The Lord Jesus Christ commands that we love as He loves.** It is not enough to say that we love, but we truly love with our actions and deeds. In the family of God we are loved by the Father and also by the brethren. No one realized this love as much as the beloved Apostle John. He firmly declares in 1st John 3:14, *We know that we have passed from death unto life, because we _____ the brethren. He that loveth not his brother abideth in death.* The Apostle John admonishes us in 1st John 3:18, *My little children, let us not love in **word**, neither in **tongue**; but in _____ and in **truth**.* It is impossible to give this too much emphasis. John even declares in 1st John 4:11-12, *Beloved, if God so loved us, we ought also to _____ one another. No man hath seen God at any time. If we love one another, God dwelleth in us, and his love is perfected in us.* Do you love the brethren in this manner? _____

8. We have **new desires, new activities, new attitudes and new goals** as a result of our salvation.

   a. God gives us a command in 1st Peter 1:14-16, that we not only have the name **saint**, but that we must **practice holy living** in obedience to God: *As obedient children, not fashioning yourselves according to the former lusts in your ignorance: But as he which hath called you is holy, so be ye holy in _____ manner of conversation* [manner of life]; *because it is written, Be ye holy; for I am holy.* Now that we are God's children, He continues to change us to be conformed to His nature. You will find that the things you did before no longer bring the same satisfaction. Things are different now! Why are these changes happening? Ephesians 2:10 explains, *For we are his workmanship, created in Christ Jesus unto _____ works, which God hath before ordained that we should walk in them.* We have a new life in Jesus Christ! Now we belong to Him and we do not belong to the world.

   b. God expects changes in our life to be visible to us and to others. Our actions should be in accord with our identification with Christ. After we have been "born again," God wants us to have a normal development in our new Christian life. We are admonished in 2nd Peter 3:18, *But _____ in grace, and in the knowledge of our Lord and Savior Jesus Christ.* The Apostle Paul also showed his desire to grow in grace and in the knowledge of the Lord when he stated in Philippians 3:13-14: *Brethren, I count not myself to have apprehended* [achieved]: *but this one thing I do, _____ those things which are behind, and reaching forth unto those things which are before,* **I press toward the mark** *for the prize of the high calling of God in Christ Jesus.* In order to grow it is necessary to daily feed upon the Word of God. Not only should we study and meditate in the Word of God, but it is very important to attend worship services where sound doctrine from the Word of God is being preached. This is extremely important.

   c. **As true Christians we will want to follow the Lord Jesus Christ,** as He said in John 10:27: *My sheep hear my voice, and I know them, and they _____ me.* Our conduct must express the life that we now have in Jesus Christ. 1st John 2:6 tells us how to live: *He that saith he abideth in Him ought himself also so to _____, even as He walked.* How did

Jesus walk? He lived in obedience to His Father! The Apostle Paul gives us the command in Romans 12:2, *Be not conformed to this world: but be ye transformed by the renewing of your _____, that ye may prove what is that good, and acceptable, and perfect, will of God.* We are reminded in Romans 8:9 that the Holy Spirit lives in us: *But ye are not in the flesh,* [living according to worldly desires] *but in the Spirit, if so be that the Spirit of God dwell in you. Now if any man have not the Spirit of Christ, he is none of his.* Is it your desire to separate yourself from a worldly life and live for Jesus Christ? _____

d. True Christian should desire that others come to know the Lord Jesus Christ as their personal Savior. Do you want to tell the world that you now belong to the Lord Jesus Christ? _____ In Romans 1:16, the Apostle Paul declared, *For I am not _____ of the Gospel of Christ: for it is the power of God unto salvation to every one that believeth; to the Jew first, and also to the Greek.* Now we are not ashamed to tell others about our conversion to Jesus Christ. We need to share the Gospel with as many as possible.

9. We have a **new promise** as a result of our salvation.

In John 14:1-3, Jesus Christ speaks of a great promise: *Let not your heart be troubled: ye believe in God, believe also in me. In my Father's house are many mansions: if it were not so, I would have told you. I go to prepare a place for you. And if I go and prepare a place for you, I will come again, and _____ you unto myself; that where I am, there ye may be also.* This passage teaches us of the reality of the return of the Lord Jesus Christ for His own. It is referred to as the "rapture" of the true Christian. The Apostle Paul explained and confirmed this in 1st Thessalonians 4:13-18. In verse 17 he says, *Then we which are alive and remain shall be caught up together with them in the clouds, to _____ the Lord in the air: and so shall we _____ be with the Lord.* This is the glorious hope and anticipation of the true Christian! We will have transformed bodies and will physically be present with Jesus Christ forever. In 1st Corinthians 2:9, the Apostle Paul exclaimed, *Eye hath not seen, nor ear heard, neither have entered into the heart of man, the things which _____ hath prepared for them that love him.*

10. We have a **personal teacher, the Holy Spirit** as the result of our salvation.

The Apostle Paul explains the ministry of the Holy Spirit in 1st Corinthians 2:12-13: *Now we have received, not the spirit of the world, but the _____ which is of God; that we might know the things that are freely given to us of God. Which things also we speak, not in the words which man's wisdom teacheth, but which the Holy Ghost teacheth; comparing spiritual things with spiritual.* This means that the Holy Spirit helps us to understand Scripture by comparing the teaching in one passage of God's Word with other passages. In this way we have a greater understanding of God's Word.

SUMMARY:

We cannot do anything to help Christ save us. As repentant sinners we can only surrender ourselves to Him with all our heart. What are the results of salvation? God brings many changes into the life of the new believer. The true Christian has a new life and belongs to a new family. He has new desires, new attitudes, new actions, and new purposes. The Christian also has new responsibilities to grow in grace and the knowledge of our Lord and Savior Jesus Christ. He will desire to live a life that is separated from sinful practices in order to be used by God. If we confess our sins to God, we know that He has forgiven us. We **know** that we are saved and secure in God's hands, and He will not let us fall. The Apostle Paul expressed his relationship with Christ in Galatians 2:20 by saying: *I am crucified with Christ: nevertheless I live; yet not I, but Christ liveth in me: and the life which I now live in the flesh I live by the faith of the Son of God, who loved me, and gave himself for me.* In Galatians 3:15, the Apostle Paul explained a great truth regarding our assurance: *Though it be but a man's covenant, yet if it be confirmed, no man disannulleth* [to cancel], *or addeth thereto.* No one can take away, improve or add to the true work that God does in our life.

REVIEW QUESTIONS – CHAPTER 6

THE ASSURANCE OF THE TRUE CHRISTIAN

1. Was it necessary for Jesus Christ to die for us? (1st Peter 3:18) _____
    Why _____
    _____

2. Are you sure that Jesus Christ has saved you? _____

3. How do you know for sure that you are saved? _____
_____

4. Upon what Bible verses do you base the assurance of your salvation? Please give the references. _____
_____

5. Will you go to Heaven when you die? _____ Will you spend all eternity with God? _____ How do you know? _____
_____

6. What is a saint? _____

7. How are we sanctified? (Hebrews 10:10) *We are sanctified through the offering of the body of Jesus Christ _____ for _____ [eternity].*

8. Do you still sin? _____ Why? _____

9. What things can separate us from the love of Christ? (Romans 8:35-39)
_____

10. What can break our **relationship with God** now that we are His sons?
_____

11. What things can break our **fellowship with God** now that we are His sons? _____

12. Is there a sin from your past that God cannot forgive? _____

13. How many times would Jesus have to die as a sacrifice for our sins? _____

14. Does there exist some ceremony, such as baptism or "the sacrifice of the mass," which can bring you "special grace," helping you to be more spiritual or making it possible to have fellowship with God? _____

15. If someone prays at least five times a day, can this practice bring him some "special grace," helping him to be more spiritual or making possible his fellowship with God? _____

16. Which sin can cause us to lose our salvation? _____

17. Can a true born again Christian willfully practice sin? (1st John 3:6)_____

18. Why was it necessary for Jesus Christ to shed His blood on the cross and not just die in some other manner? (John 3:14-15; Galatians 3:13; Hebrews 9:22)
_____

19. According to Proverbs 28:13, what two things should a believer do when he sins? 1.) _____
    2.) _____

20. When a Christian sins, but does not want to recognize it, much less confess it, nor ask forgiveness from God, what will happen? (Hebrews 12:5-11)
    _____

21. For what purposes does God apply discipline to the Christian? _____
    _____
    _____

22. When Jesus said in John 10:27, *My sheep hear my voice, and I know them, and they follow me*, who are His sheep? _____
    Who is the Shepherd? _____

23. What does Jesus Christ promise in John 10:28? _____
    _____

24. What does Jesus Christ promise in John 10:29? _____
    _____

25. When the believer is at the Judgment Seat of Christ, for what things will he give an account? (2nd Corinthians 5:10) _____
    _____

26. Is it possible for the true believer to be condemned to hell? _____
    How do you know? (Romans 8:1) _____
    _____

27. Please memorize John 10:27-29 and express it in your own words. _____
    _____
    _____
    _____

Why do some Christians overcome temptations to sin and others fail? The next chapter will help you understand this.

Chapter Seven

Power to Overcome Temptations and Trials

There hath no temptation taken you but such as is common to man: but God is faithful, who will not suffer you to be tempted above that ye are able; but will with the temptation also make a way to escape, that ye may be able to bear it.
1st Corinthians 10:13

WHEN WE BECOME TRUE CHRISTIANS WE ENTER A BATTLEFIELD.

God wants us to know that we will have daily battles confronting us in our Christian life. The Apostle Peter warns us in 1st Peter 5:8-9, *Be sober, be vigilant; because **your adversary the devil, as a roaring lion,** walketh about, seeking whom he may _____: whom resist stedfast in the faith, knowing that the same afflictions are accomplished in your brethren that are in the world.* The Apostle Paul gave his young co-worker, Timothy, wise counsel in 2nd Timothy 2:3-4: *Thou therefore endure hardness, as a good _____ of Jesus Christ. No man that warreth entangleth himself with the affairs of this life; that he may please Him who hath chosen him to be a soldier.* God has called us to a life of discipline, separation, and holiness, not to a worldly life.

This is not a normal battle, nor a normal battlefield. Here the enemy attacks from all sides. We see this illustrated by an attack in the life of the Apostle Peter. He fell into Satan's trap when he expressed his own desires and personal feelings regarding what the Lord had said. As a result, the Lord Jesus Christ strongly reprimanded him in Matthew 16:21-23: *From that time forth began Jesus to shew unto his disciples, how that he must go unto Jerusalem, and suffer many things of the elders and chief priests and scribes, and be killed, and be raised again the third day. Then Peter took him, and began to rebuke him, saying, "Be it far from thee, Lord: this shall not be unto thee." But he turned, and said unto Peter, "Get thee behind me, _____: thou art an offence unto me: for thou savourest* [comprehend] *not the things that be of God, but those that be of men."* How often are we being an offence to Christ, thinking that we are doing something special for Him?

Our enemies cannot be entirely eliminated or destroyed. In Ephesians 6:12 we read, *For we wrestle not against flesh and blood, but against principalities, against powers, against the _____ of the darkness of this world, against spiritual wickedness in high places.* **This is a lifelong battle.** Our victories are from moment to moment and from day to day. Only when the Lord Jesus Christ comes to take us home to be with Him will we experience complete victory. We have to trust Jesus Christ, and give Him thanks for every victory. The Apostle Paul confidently expressed in 1ˢᵗ Corinthians 15:57, *But thanks be to God, which giveth us the _____ through our Lord Jesus Christ.*

I. THERE ARE THREE PRINCIPAL ENEMIES OF THE CHRISTIAN: THE WORLD, THE FLESH AND THE DEVIL.

The Bible teaches us that these enemies attack the Christian from three different directions to provoke us to sin.

1. The **world** tempts us to sin.

    a. We live in a perverse and sinful world that deceives and attacks the believer when least expected. The Bible makes reference to this in many passages. One way the world attacks the believer is through **materialism**. The material things of this worldly system are a strong attraction to the eyes and thoughts of many Christians. Almost all evil is related to and rotating around the love of money and possessions. The Apostle Paul carefully gives counsel to his fellow partner in 1ˢᵗ Timothy 6:9-10: *But they that will be rich fall into temptation and a snare, and into* *many foolish and hurtful lusts, which drown men in destruction and perdition. For the _____ of money is the root of all evil: which while some coveted after, they have erred from the faith, and pierced themselves through with many sorrows.* The worldly attractions such as prestige, financial success, materialism, vile worldly entertainments, vices and sinful habits are powerful temptations. All these things try to invade the life of the Christian. What command does God give to the Christian as to worldly things? The Apostle John in 1st John 2:15 admonishes, *Love not the _____, neither the things that are in the world.* He continues to give us the reason why we cannot love those things: *If any man love the world, the _____ of the Father is not in him.* The **world** refers to the sinful system, which robs us of our love for God. James 4:4 warns all those who claim to be worldly Christians: *Ye adulterers and adulteresses, know ye not that the friendship of the world is enmity with God? whosoever therefore will be a _____ of the world is the _____ of God.* This misdirected love can destroy one's desire for the things of God.

b. A person that participates in **worldly things**, and at the same time believes that he belongs to God, is deceiving himself. It is impossible to deceive God. 1st John 2:3-4 identifies the person that pretends to be a child of God, but does not obey His Word: *Hereby we do know that we know him, if we keep his commandments. He that saith, I know him, and keepeth not his commandments, is a _____, and the truth is not in him.* Again the Apostle John declares in 1st John 3:8, *He that committeth* [practices] *sin is of the devil.* 1st John 3:9 presents the positive side: *Whosoever is born of God doth not commit* [practice] *sin; for his seed remaineth in him: and he cannot* [practice] *sin, because he is born of God.* God's desire is that we live a life pleasing to Him and has made provision for us when we sin. The Word of God teaches that it is necessary to repent and confess our sins to Jesus Christ in order to have an intimate relationship with Him.

c. There are many **opposing factors** that can discourage the believer. Opposition often comes from our colleagues and friends, but the greatest opposition many times comes from the members of our own family as was predicted by Jesus Christ in Luke 12:51: *Suppose ye that I am come to give peace on earth? I tell you,*

Nay; but rather _____ *: for from henceforth there shall be five in one house divided, three against two, and two against three. The father shall be divided against the son, and the son against the father; the mother against the daughter, and the daughter against the mother; the mother-in-law against her daughter-in-law, and the daughter-in-law against her mother-in-law.* Sometimes family members turn against one of their very own, because they oppose their conversion to Jesus Christ. They see it as a threat to their religion and their way of living.

2. The **flesh** tempts us to sin.

   a. When we give ourselves to Jesus Christ, we receive a new nature that comes from God; however, we will always have to battle against our old sinful nature. The Bible refers to this sinful nature as the "flesh." In Galatians 5:17, the Apostle Paul mentions a great conflict between the two natures of the believer: *For the flesh lusteth against the Spirit, and the Spirit against the flesh: and these are* _____ *the one to the other: so that ye cannot do the things that ye would.* This conflict exists in different ways in all of us. The things that tempt one Christian will not necessarily tempt another. If we act in the flesh, we are our own worst enemy! Many activities related to the old nature are mentioned in Galatians 5:19-21. This list ends by stating, *they which do such things shall **not inherit the kingdom of God.***

   We do not just fall into sin, but there is a progressive decision to gradually move in that direction when being governed or prompted by our own fleshly desires. The solution to this problem is found in the spiritual qualities that characterize our new life in Christ, as mentioned by the Apostle Paul in Galatians 5:22-25: *But the* _____ *of the Spirit is love, joy, peace, longsuffering, gentleness, goodness, faith, meekness, temperance: against such there is no law. And they that are Christ's have crucified the flesh with the affections and lusts.* This list finishes with the declaration, *If we live in the Spirit, let us also* _____ *in the Spirit.*

   b. Why is there so much wickedness in the heart of mankind? The answer is found in Jeremiah 17:9: *The heart is* _____ *above all things, and desperately wicked: who can know it?* The sinful heart is controlling the fleshly desires of sinful man. The

Apostle Paul warned Timothy, in 2nd Timothy 3:1-7, against dangerous people who desire to have a negative influence in the life of the Christian: *This know also, that in the last days _____ times shall come. For men shall be lovers of their own selves, covetous, boasters, proud, blasphemers, disobedient to parents, unthankful, unholy, without natural affection, trucebreakers, false accusers, incontinent, fierce, despisers of those that are good, traitors, heady, high-minded, lovers of pleasures more than lovers of God; having a form of godliness, but denying the power thereof: from such turn away. For of this sort are they which creep into houses, and lead captive silly women laden with sins, led away with divers lusts, ever learning, and never able to come to the knowledge of the truth.* We have to be on guard against all this wickedness.

c. The Apostle Paul clearly teaches what God expects us to do regarding our former way of life. It is important to recognize the way we lived in the past and drastically correct it. We cannot be friendly with the three principle enemies of our soul (the world, the flesh and the devil), thinking that with time they will stop attacking us. Colossians 3:5-7 commands, *mortify* [make die] *therefore your members which are upon the earth* [the worldly life]*; fornication, uncleanness, inordinate affection, evil concupiscence, and covetousness, which is idolatry: For which things' sake the _____ of God cometh on the children of disobedience: In the which ye also walked some time, when ye lived in them.* The phrase *mortify therefore your members*, has reference to a constant effort of putting sin to death. It is like weeding a garden. Even though we carefully try to pull up the weeds with the roots, they continue to come up again. In the same way, putting sin to death does not happen once for all, but is a continual action. We have to make a firm decision to continually put an end to worldly practices in our life, since worldliness is an enemy of God. Many times people blame the devil for the problems in their life, when in reality it is the result of their own sinful fleshly desires. The Apostle Paul, in Ephesians 4:22, forcefully insisted, *That ye put off concerning the _____ conversation* [manner of life] *the old man, which is corrupt according to the deceitful lusts.* Are you being overcome with fleshly desires and temptations in your life? Examine carefully your heart, look for the solution according to God's Word, and then take the necessary measures to correct your ways.

3. The **devil** (Satan) tempts us to sin.

    a. The devil is our major enemy. Satan wants to trip us and make us fall. For this reason the Apostle Paul, in 2nd Corinthians 2:11, insisted that we recognize Satan's tactics: *Lest Satan should get an advantage of us: for we are not _____ of his devices.* For our own protection we have to be careful to obey the command that the Apostle Paul gave in Ephesians 4:27: *Neither give place to the devil.* We should never try to resist the devil in our own strength; however, we must first submit ourselves to God, as it teaches in James 4:6-8: *But he giveth more grace. Wherefore he saith, God resisteth the proud, but giveth grace unto the humble. _____ yourselves therefore to God. Resist the devil, and he will flee from you. Draw nigh to God, and he will draw nigh to you. Cleanse your hands, ye sinners; and purify your hearts, ye double minded.*

    b. Satan transforms himself into an "angel of light" with the purpose of deceiving people. Just because many use the Bible, don't be deceived by thinking that they are teaching the truth, for there are many false teachers and preachers who teach things that appear to be good and helpful; however, they distort the truth with error. The Apostle Paul declares in 2nd Corinthians 11:13-15, *For such are false apostles, deceitful workers, transforming themselves into the apostles of Christ. And no marvel; for Satan himself is _____ into an* **angel of light**. *Therefore it is no great thing if his ministers also be transformed as the ministers of righteousness; whose end shall be according to their works.* Satan wants to deceive us, mislead us and discourage us by putting snares in our path. Eve listened to him and was deceived. This is the reason the Apostle Paul shows extreme concern in 2nd Corinthians 11:3: *But I fear, lest by any means, as the serpent beguiled Eve through his subtilty, **so your minds should be corrupted** from the simplicity that is in Christ.* The tragic result would be the abandonment of our simple devotion to Christ in favor of the sophisticated error of false teachings. Satan wants to attack our senses and destroy our capacity to reason. He can do it through people, music, activities, amusements or other attractions. God wants us to be centered in the Word of God, which is our defense.

II. THE BIBLE TEACHES THE CHRISTIAN HOW TO HAVE VICTORY OVER THE WORLD, THE FLESH AND THE DEVIL.

1. We should recognize our weaknesses and our inability to overcome sin without God's help.

    a. On occasions we can overcome temptations and trials by our own strength; however, most of the time we will fail. Satan, our enemy, wants us to think that we are able to do it without God's help. The Apostle Paul warns in 1st Corinthians 10:12, *Wherefore let him that _____ he standeth take heed lest he fall.* If we submit ourselves to Jesus Christ we have the assurance of victory, because He dwells in us. Ephesians 3:20 also assures us that Christ *is able to do exceeding abundantly above all that we ask or think according to the _____ that worketh in us.*

    b. Even though we are weak, God assures us in 1st John 4:4, that we have His help: *Ye are of God, little children, and have overcome them: because _____ is he that is in you, than he that is in the world.* Romans 8:31 instructs us to put God first in our life and He will help us: *What shall we then say to these things? If God be for us, _____ can be against us?* Here is the important question! Is God in favor of what you are doing and the manor in which you are living? _____ If your answer is "No," you should correct your way of living and be obedient to God's Word. The testimony given by the Apostle Paul, in Romans 8:35-39, has been an encouragement to many Christians: *Who shall _____ us from the love of Christ? shall tribulation, or distress, or persecution, or famine, or nakedness, or peril, or sword? As it is written, for thy sake we are killed all the day long; we are accounted as sheep for the slaughter. Nay, in all these things we are more than conquerors through him that loved us. For I am _____, that neither death, nor life, nor angels, nor principalities, nor powers, nor things present, nor things to come, nor height, nor depth, nor any other creature, shall be able to _____ us from the love of God, which is in Christ Jesus our Lord.*

107

c. We must equip ourselves with all the armor of God in order to have victory as true soldiers of Jesus Christ. Ephesians 6:10-18 gives us a list of provisions that we need in order to combat the attacks of Satan and *the rulers of the darkness of this world.* Verse 11 gives us the command: *Put on the _____ armor of God, that ye may be able to stand against the wiles* [strategies] *of the devil.* We cannot be indifferent to any part of this armor. All of the armor is important! It is the permanent attire of the Christian to be used the rest of his life. In love God has provided it for us.

2. We must recognize our sin, confess our sin, and ask God for forgiveness.

   a. We cannot ignore sin in our life. When we realize that we have sinned against God, we must be quick to humble ourselves and confess our sins to Him. 1st John 1:8 declares, *If **we say** that we have no sin, we deceive ourselves, and the truth is not in us.* The Apostle John includes himself in this whole passage to let us know that no one is exempt from sin, and no one can deceive God. Also, verse 10 teaches, *If we say that we have not _____, we make him a liar, and his word is not in us.* The reason many people do not give importance to sin is because they are minimizing it, considering it to be only a mistake. It is important to recognize all sin is direct rebellion against God and His Word.

   b. We are commanded in 1st John 1:9 to confess our sin and ask God for forgiveness: *If we _____ our sins, he is faithful and just to forgive us our sins, and to cleanse us from all unrighteousness.* **Confession** means – "to say the same thing, or be in agreement." In this case it talks about being in agreement with God regarding our sin. God wants us to agree with Him regarding what He says about our sins, and see them as He does. It is not just admitting that we have done something wrong, but to truly repent of our sin and recognize that we have offended God.

3. We have to trust God for His protection and victories.

   a. God has the power to deliver us from all temptations that come our way. He promises us in Hebrews 2:18, *For in that he himself hath suffered being _____, he is able to succor* [give help to] *them that are tempted.* We must always remember the promise from God's Word in 2nd Thessalonians 3:3: *But the Lord is faithful, who shall stablish you, and _____ you from evil.*

b. If one willfully goes against God, he leaves the umbrella of God's protection and is vulnerable to Satan's attacks. It is always our personal responsibility to submit to God. Only in this way will we have the strength to resist the devil. James 4:7-8 commands, *Submit yourselves therefore to God. Resist the devil, and he will flee from you. Draw nigh to God, and he will draw nigh to you. Cleanse your hands, ye sinners; and _____ your hearts, ye double minded.* To **submit** is the act of surrendering to the authority of God as the Sovereign ruler over our life. The way in which we combat Satan is taught in Ephesians 6:10-18, and is summed up in verse 13: *Wherefore take unto you the **whole** armor of God, that ye may be able to withstand in the evil day, and having done all, to stand.*

c. God is faithful to protect us from the temptations that we are not able to resist. Our memory verse in 1st Corinthians 10:13 promises, *God is faithful, who will not suffer* [permit] *you to be tempted above that ye are able; but will with the temptation also make a way to _____, that ye may be able to bear it.* He will not leave us defenseless. In 2nd Peter 2:9, the Apostle Peter wrote, *The Lord knoweth how to _____ the godly* [the true Christian] *out of temptation, and to reserve the unjust unto the day of judgment to be punished.* The Lord Jesus Christ is trustworthy! The Apostle Paul expressed his gratitude to God in 2nd Corinthians 2:14: *Now thanks be unto God, which always causeth us to _____ in Christ.* We should give thanks to God for His protection and victories that we receive each day.

4. We have to be fortified by the Word of God.

a. It is necessary for us to **read and study God's Word** in order to help us have victory over the temptations and trials that come our way. The Apostle John writes in 1st John 2:14, *I have written unto you, fathers, because ye have known him that is from the beginning. I have written unto you, young men, because ye are strong, and the word of God abideth* [lives] *in you, and ye have _____ the wicked one.* It is so very important to be diligent in the study of God's Word. 2nd Timothy 2:15 commands us to, *Study to shew thyself approved unto God, a workman that* *needeth not to be ashamed, _____ dividing the word of truth.* We are to rightly compare Scripture with Scripture as we study and teach God's Word.

b. It is essential for us to **meditate in God's Word** to help us have victory over the temptations that come our way. We should set aside time every day for individual and family devotions to read the Bible and pray. God exhorts us in Deuteronomy 6:6-7, *And these words, which I command thee this day, shall be in thine _____: And thou shalt teach them diligently unto thy children, and shalt talk of them when thou sittest in thine house, and when thou walkest by the way, and when thou liest down, and when thou risest up.* In Joshua 1:8, God exhorted Joshua to faithfully meditate in His Word: *This book of the law shall not depart out of thy mouth; but thou shalt meditate therein day and night, that thou mayest observe to do according to all that is written therein: for then thou shalt make thy way prosperous, and then thou shalt have good success.* It is not enough to know the Word of God, but to practice the things that we learn.

c. It is very important for us to **memorize key verses in God's Word** to help us have victory over the temptations that come our way. In Psalm 119:11, the psalmist expressed his purpose for memorizing the Word of God: *Thy word have I hid in mine _____, that I might not sin against thee.* Another purpose for the memorization of God's Word is to stand firm in our spiritual life. Psalm 37:31 states, *The law of his God is in his _____; none of his steps shall slide.*

5. We have to watch and pray.

a. It is more than a mere suggestion to watch and pray, because we are in a war it is our responsibility to *watch* and be alert as soldiers. In Matthew 26:41, Jesus Christ warns: _____ *and pray, that ye enter not into temptation: the spirit indeed is willing, but the flesh is weak.* The Apostle Paul admonished the brethren in 1st Corinthians 16:13-14, as to how to confront the dangers that they are facing: *Watch ye, _____ fast in the faith, quit you like men* [act like men]*, be strong. Let all your things be done with charity* [love]*.* He is telling us not to give up or give in to the pressures of this world, but to press on, knowing that our help comes from the Lord.

110

b. We have an example in Colossians 1:9-10 of the Apostle Paul **praying** for the believers: *For this cause we also, since the day we heard it, do not cease to _____for you, and to desire that ye might be filled with the knowledge of his will in all wisdom and spiritual understanding; that ye might walk worthy of the Lord unto all pleasing, being fruitful in every good work, and increasing in the knowledge of God.* Being tempted is not a sin in itself; however, when we yield to temptation it is sin. Ephesians 6:18 admonishes us to pray for one another: *Praying always with _____ prayer and supplication in the Spirit, and watching thereunto with _____ perseverance and supplication for ____ saints.* We must dedicate time to **pray** for the needs of others, that they will have God's strength and His wisdom for every situation.

6. It is important that we faithfully attend a church where they teach and practice the sound doctrines of the Bible.

   a. We must faithfully **hear the preaching and teaching of God's Word** in order to grow spiritually and have His direction in our life. If we do not attend church, we will be in direct disobedience to God's mandate. Hebrews 10:25-26 gives the command: *Not forsaking the assembling of ourselves _____, as the manner of some is; but exhorting one another: and so much the more, as ye see the day approaching. For if we sin willfully after that we have received the knowledge of the truth, there remaineth no more sacrifice for sins.* As we read in verse 26, to not attend church services and miss the teaching of God's Word is an act of voluntary sin. On the other hand, if we are faithful in church attendance we will become grounded in His Word and God will bless us. We need the teachings and counsel from a pastor that is faithful to Jesus Christ and His Word.

   b. It is vital that we **grow in grace by reading and studying the Word of God** in order to strengthen our walk with the Lord. We are admonished in 2nd Peter 3:18, *But _____ in grace, and in the knowledge of our Lord and Savior Jesus Christ. To him be glory both now and for ever. Amen.* There are many ways to grow in our spiritual life. I will mention some.

      1) Sit toward the front of the church to avoid distractions.
      2) Take thorough notes of the messages.

3) Later, find time to review your notes and Bible passages from the messages.

4) When you have doubts or need clarification you should ask for the pastor's help at an opportune time.

5) You need to put into practice what you learn.

6) Share your testimony and the Word of God with others. This is a command given by Jesus Christ and also your spiritual exercise!

III. THE BIBLE GIVES THE BASIS FOR THE SEPARATION OF THE CHRISTIAN.

God commands Christians to live a life of personal separation – separation from the worldly system, and separation to God in our daily living. Personal separation includes the believer's rejection of his old sinful passions. Time and time again we are warned in Scripture that *whosoever will be a friend of the _____ is the enemy of God.* (James 4:4)

1. The Bible clearly admonishes us to be **separated from the worldly system, worldly activities and worldly things.**

    a. God's Word insists that there be a distinct difference between those who have given themselves to Jesus Christ and those who belong to their father, Satan. In John 17:16, Jesus Christ prayed to His Father, *They are not of the _____ , even as I am not of the world.* The attitude of the world is one of pride and egotism, desiring riches and fame. Humility is the least of the things on their mind. The spirit of this world cannot be in agreement or in harmony with the Spirit of God. We find a very important question in Amos 3:3 regarding our separation: *Can two walk together, except they be _____?* If we are truly in agreement with God and sincerely love Him, we cannot defraud Him by loving the worldly system in which we live!

    b. In Galatians 5:16-18, the Apostle Paul warns the Christians against living a sensual and worldly life: *This I say then, walk in the Spirit, and ye shall not fulfill the _____ of the flesh.* It is an impossibility to live in fleshly lusts and at the same time walk in conformity to the Spirit of God. We are either spiritual or worldly. How does God want us to live? _____ In Galatians 5:19-21, the Apostle Paul presents a list of characteristics and practices of this worldly system which God hates: *Adultery, fornication, uncleanness, lasciviousness, idolatry, witchcraft, hatred, variance, emulations, wrath, strife, seditions, heresies, envyings, murders, drunkenness, revellings, and such like: of the which I tell you before, as I have also told you in time past,* **that they which do such things shall_____ inherit the Kingdom of God.** Are those who practice these sins condemned to eternal judgment, or are they just "worldly Christians?" _____

_____

c. If our thoughts and desires are dedicated to temporal and earthly things, then how can we truthfully say that we love God? Many of those who say that they love God do not show it. 1st John 2:15-16 exhorts the brethren, *Love not the world, neither the things that are in the world. If any man love the world, the love of the_____ is not in him. For all that is in the world, the lust of the flesh, and the lust of the eyes, and the pride of life, is not of the Father, but is of the_____.* The desires of the true Christian should not be toward carnal things, such as the movie theater, television, dancing, the use of tobacco and alcohol, all of which lead to worldly parties with illicit sex, immoral activities, pornography, drugs, etc. The wrong use of the tongue is an offense to God, by lying, using bad words, slander and blasphemy. How can we love God and at the same time love and participate in deplorable sensual practices? If we truly love God we cannot defraud Him.

d. God condemns our association with the "works of darkness." In 2nd Corinthians 6:14-17, God gives an order that we must obey in every area of our life: *Be ye not unequally yoked* [joined] *together with _____: for what fellowship hath righteousness with unrighteousness? and what communion* [fellowship] *hath light with darkness* [the dominion of Satan]? *And what concord* [harmony] *hath Christ with Belial* [Satan]? *or what part hath he that believeth with an infidel* [an unbeliever]? *And what agreement hath the temple of God with idols? for ye are the temple of the living God; as God hath said, I will dwell in them, and walk in them; and I will be their God, and they shall be my people. Wherefore come out from among them, and be ye _____, saith the Lord, and touch not the unclean thing; and I will receive you, and will be a Father unto you, and ye shall be my sons and daughters, saith the Lord Almighty.* If you belong to God, you cannot continue your sinful life of the past. Has God changed your life? _____ How has God changed you? _____

_____

e. Those who do not belong to Jesus Christ love the world and what it has to offer. They choose worldly friends and follow the immodest and immoral styles of the world. Parents need to be modest in their dress and behavior to be that Christian example for others and especially their own children. So many are in agreement with worldly standards, and enjoy the world's frivolousness and entertainments. Is it possible for a person to be a Christian and at the same time waste his life in the pursuit of lustful worldly pleasures of sin? _____ Those who practice sin show no evidence of having been born again. Remember the warning in Ecclesiastes 12:14: *For God shall bring every work into judgment, with every _____ thing, whether it be good or whether it be evil.* In no way can we live according to the desires of the flesh and at the same time live according to the Spirit of God. James 4:4 clearly states that we cannot belong to two worlds: *Ye adulterers and adulteresses, know ye not that the friendship of the world is enmity with God? Whosoever therefore will be a friend of the world is the _____ of God.* If you are a friend of the world you are an enemy of our Lord Jesus Christ!

2. The Bible admonishes us to be **separated unto God as His instruments of righteousness.**

a. In contrast to a life that was dominated by the world and worldly desires, the true Christian has an abundant life with great blessings and many opportunities to please God as he walks in true fellowship with Christ. Romans 8:6 declares, *For to be carnally minded is death. but to be spiritually minded is _____ and peace.* Separation from worldly practices to God is one of the evidences that we love Jesus Christ and belong to Him. In 2nd Corinthians 7:1, the Apostle Paul gives very important instructions to every child of God: *Having therefore these promises, dearly beloved, let us _____ ourselves from all filthiness of the flesh and spirit, perfecting holiness in the fear of God.*

b. The separation of ourselves from worldly practices gives us only one option – we must be separated to God and live for Him. This separation is not isolation, but involves our being obedient to everything that is taught in God's Word. Our actions show that we love God and we will see spiritual growth and maturity in our life. The Apostle Paul gave the command in Romans 6:12-13, *Let not sin therefore reign in your mortal body, that ye should _____ it in the lusts thereof. Neither _____ ye your members as instruments of unrighteousness unto sin: but yield yourselves unto God, as those that are alive from the dead, and your members as instruments of righteousness unto God.* We cannot expect the world to appreciate our firm stand for Christ and His Word. In John 17:14-20, we see the concern of the Lord Jesus Christ as He was praying to God the Father for those who had placed their full trust in Him: *I have given them thy word; and the world hath _____ them, because they are not of the world, even as I am not of the world. I pray not that thou shouldest take them out of the world, but that thou shouldest keep them from the evil* [the evil one, Satan]. *They are not of the world, even as I am not of the world. Sanctify them through thy truth: thy word is truth. As thou hast sent me into the world, even so have I also sent them into the world. And for their sakes I sanctify myself, that they also might be sanctified through the truth.* [Jesus Christ sanctified Himself, set Himself apart, to be that example that we might also set ourselves apart for Him and His ministry.] *Neither pray I for these alone, but for them also which shall believe on me through their word.* His purpose for leaving us in the world is that we be His witnesses.

c. It is very important that each one of us examine our heart regarding our associations, activities, attitudes, thoughts, what we see, what we hear, what we do and also, how we dress in the light of the Word of God. A person who belongs to this worldly system lives for this world. We cannot expect him to do anything else, because that is his way of life, his person, his character and his very nature. The Christian has a different Spirit, the Holy Spirit, who lives in him. 1st Corinthians 2:12 affirms this truth: *Now we have received, not the spirit of the world, but the Spirit which is of _____.* The Apostle Paul identifies the true Christian in 2nd Timothy 2:19: *Nevertheless the foundation of God standeth sure, having this seal, the Lord knoweth them that are His. And, let every one that nameth the name of Christ _____ from iniquity* [sin]. Matthew 6:24 says, *No man can serve two masters: for either* he will _____ the one, and _____ the other; or else he will *hold to the one, and despise the other. Ye cannot serve God and mammon.* The word, "serve" is very important, because the will of God is that we only serve Him. God asks for our faithfulness to Him; however, God will not impose His will on us. He asks that we faithfully live a separated life for Him in every way.

d. We need to separate ourselves to those things that will produce holiness in our life. In 1st Peter 1:16, God requires holiness in our life: *Be ye holy; for I am holy.* How is this accomplished? The Apostle Peter tells us in verse 13, *Wherefore gird up the loins of your _____, be sober, and hope* [we look forward] *to the end for the grace that is to be brought unto you at the revelation of Jesus Christ.* **First**, we need to discipline our mind to think correctly. **Second**, we need to take the responsibility for our actions. **Third**, we must focus our expectations on God's grace. **Fourth**, there has to be a direct rejection of worldly lifestyles and thought patterns, including our "former lusts," that enslaved us before our conversion. This is confirmed in verse 14: *As obedient children, not fashioning yourselves according to the _____ lusts in your ignorance.* In Romans 12:1-2, the Apostle Paul pleads with the Christians: *I beseech you therefore, brethren, by the mercies of God, that ye present your bodies a living sacrifice, holy, acceptable unto God, which is your reasonable service. And be not _____ to this world: but be ye* **transformed by the renewing of your mind,** *that ye may prove what is that good, and acceptable, and perfect, will of God.* Has your mind and thinking been truly transformed by Jesus Christ, or are you still occupied with the trash of this worldly system?

3. The Bible clearly commands us to be **separated from the religious traditions** we practiced before we were converted.

a. Idolatry is evil and a great sin in God's eyes. Read Exodus 20:3-5: *Thou shalt have no other gods before me. Thou shalt not make unto thee any graven _____, or any likeness of any thing that is in Heaven above, or that is in the earth beneath, or that is in the water under the earth. Thou shalt not bow down thyself to them, nor serve them: for I the Lord thy God am a jealous God, visiting the iniquity of the fathers upon the children unto the third and fourth generation of them that hate me.* (Other important passages

116

dealing with this same subject are Psalm 115:3-8; Psalm 135:15-18; Habakkuk 2:18-20 and Deuteronomy 7:25.) God prohibits anything that could take His place, such as images, persons, places or relics that we previously worshiped. The Bible teaches that we should never pray to any person, such as the Virgin Mary, angels or what some esteem as "saints," Those practices have to be discarded or you are acting in direct disobedience to God. If you have them in your house or life they should be destroyed.

b. God requires that we be separated from the contamination of this world, both moral and spiritual, as we read in Romans 12:1-2. This act of giving ourselves to God is again emphasized in 2nd Corinthians 6:17-18: *Wherefore come out from among them, and be ye _____, saith the Lord, and touch not the unclean thing; and I will receive you. And will be a Father unto you, and ye shall be my sons and daughters, saith the Lord Almighty.* If our body belongs to God, how is it possible to give to the world that which belongs to God? The Apostle warns in 3rd John 1:11, *Beloved, follow not that which is evil, but that which is good. He that doeth _____ is of God: but he that doeth evil hath not seen God.* He is evil! He has not seen God work in his life, nor does he belong to God!

c. Giving heed to false teachers is extremely dangerous. God wants us to be faithful to the pure, holy and sound doctrine of the Word of God. 2nd Timothy 4:3-4 predicts, *For the time will come when they will _____ endure sound doctrine; but after their own lusts* [carnal desires] *shall they heap to themselves teachers, having itching ears; And they shall turn away their ears from the truth, and shall be turned unto fables.* In 2nd Corinthians 11:3, the Apostle Paul begs the Corinthians not to permit their minds to be corrupted by Satan: *But I fear, lest by any means, as the serpent beguiled Eve through his subtilty, so your _____ should be corrupted from the simplicity* [sincere fidelity] *that is in Christ.* The Apostle Paul warns, in 2nd Corinthians 11:4, about those who preach error: *For if he that cometh preacheth another _____, whom we have not preached, or if ye receive another spirit, which ye have not received, or another Gospel, which ye have not accepted, ye might well bear with him.* Colossians 2:8 warns, *Beware lest any man spoil you* [mislead you] *through*

117

philosophy and vain deceit, after the traditions of men, after the rudiments of the world, and _____ after Christ.

4.   The Bible clearly admonishes us **to practice ecclesiastical separation.**

Ecclesiastical separation has reference to doctrinal separation. Sound biblical doctrine is to be preserved by the local church, while false doctrine is to be identified, very definitely rejected and avoided. Doctrinal separation can be explained in two aspects:

a.   **We are to separate ourselves from those individuals who teach true doctrine mixed with error.** This is a satanic tactic beginning in the Garden of Eden. We are to separate ourselves from those who teach false doctrines. There is no room for dialogue and much less compromise. The Apostle Paul explains, in Romans 16:17, what should be done with those who cause doctrinal problems: *Now I beseech you, brethren, mark them which cause divisions and offenses contrary to the doctrine which ye have learned; and _____ them.* The Apostle John confirms this same teaching, in 2ⁿᵈ John 1:7 and 9-11: *For many deceivers are entered into the world, . . . Whosoever transgresseth, and abideth not in the doctrine of Christ, hath not God. He that abideth in the doctrine of Christ, he hath both the Father and the Son. If there come any unto you, and bring not this doctrine, **receive him not into your** _____**, neither bid him God speed**: For he that biddeth him God speed is partaker of his evil deeds.* It is important to reject them and their literature.

True biblical separation is a matter of love –
• **a love for God** that rejects this worldly system,
• **a love for the church** that will not tolerate false teachers who desire to lead the sheep astray and to devour them,
• **a love for Christian brethren,**
• **a love that is willing to endure,** even a break in fellowship in order to help the brother to correct his ways.

This is clearly taught in Matthew 18:15-17. Separation is not an end in itself; rather with patience, restoration should be our goal as Galatians 6:1 teaches: *Brethren, if a man be overtaken in a fault, ye which are spiritual, _____ such an one in the spirit of meekness; considering thyself, lest thou also be tempted.*

b. We are to separate ourselves from organized "apostate Christianity." The danger of this apostasy is evident in many churches as they continue to be engulfed by worldly influences and the organization of the "One World Church." It is sad to see so many churches dilute the Gospel message and minimize basic doctrines, which are vital to salvation and the faithful walk of the Christian. The Apostle Paul warned in 1ˢᵗ Timothy 4:1-3, what will happen in the future: *Now the _____ speaketh expressly, that in the latter times some shall depart from the faith, giving heed to seducing spirits, and doctrines of devils; speaking lies in hypocrisy; having their conscience seared with a hot iron; forbidding to marry, and commanding to abstain from meats, which God hath created to be received with thanksgiving of them which believe and know the truth.* Beware of the trend, which introduces worldly music, entertainment and worldly practices into the church in their effort to make the Gospel compatible to the world.

In his practice of personal separation, the true Christian must recognize the teachings that are wrong and unscriptural. We are instructed in Titus 1:13 what we must do: *This witness is true. Wherefore _____ them sharply, that they may be sound in the faith.* In doing so, we should not become frustrated or vindictive. Ecclesiastical separation also involves separation from false teachers and from the false teachings found in many so-called "Christian" books. The Bible foretells in 2ⁿᵈ Peter 2:1, that there will be those who will depart from the faith and will continue to bring destructive heresies into the church: *But there were false prophets also among the people, even as there shall be _____ teachers among you, who privily* [secretly] *shall bring in damnable heresies, even denying the Lord that bought them, and bring upon themselves swift destruction.* In Acts 20:29-30, the Apostle Paul challenged the leaders of the Ephesian church to be on guard for themselves and for the church, because false teachers would enter into the church, and other false teachers would arise from within the church. In 2ⁿᵈ Timothy 3:5, the Apostle Paul admonished Timothy to turn away from those who have a form of godliness, but deny its power. In 2ⁿᵈ John 1:9-11, the Apostle John even forbade Christians from inviting false teachers into their homes, lest believers become partakers in their evil deeds. The local church must not cooperate with people who pervert biblical doctrine; instead, the local church must identify and reject deceitful false teachers. There must be no compromise with those who twist and distort God's Word! Jude 1:3 declares, *It was needful for me to write unto you, and exhort you that ye should earnestly _____ for the faith which was once delivered unto the saints.* We must take a stand, no matter what the cost or sacrifice may be! God holds you responsible for defending and maintaining "sound doctrine" in your personal life and the church.

IV. WHAT GUIDELINES DO WE FIND IN THE BIBLE REGARDING QUESTIONABLE ACTIVITIES?

There are six important questions that serve as guidelines when the Bible is not clear whether an activity is inappropriate and wrong for us or not. We know that God speaks clearly about many things such as, *be not drunk with wine,* found in Ephesians 5:18. There is no doubt about the command given in 1st Corinthians 6:18, *Flee fornication.* In these cases we are morally bound to obey, but what does the Bible teach about activities that are doubtful? What should we do regarding things that are not specifically mentioned in the Bible? **When there is doubt, ask yourself the following questions:**

1. **Does this thing or activity support or go against the general message of the Bible,** even though there is no Scripture that mentions it? The Apostle Paul declares in 1st Corinthians 10:23, *All things* [referring to those things which are good] *are lawful for me, but all things are not expedient* [convenient]*: all things are lawful for me, but all things edify not* [do not build up]. Am I convinced by the Word of God that I am doing the right thing?

2. **Is this activity really necessary?** Hebrews 12:1 states, *Wherefore seeing we also are compassed about with so great a cloud of witnesses, let us lay aside every **weight**, and the sin which doth so easily beset us, and let us run with patience the race that is set before us.* Are the things or activities in which I am participating a "weight" on my life so that I cannot serve the Lord Jesus Christ as I should?

3. **Is this activity helpful for my spiritual life and the spiritual life of others?** Under grace we are free, but we should use our freedom to make good decisions. A good decision is one that pleases God

and is beneficial to all. In short, a good decision is one that reflects my love toward God and others. We see this rule of love described in Romans 14:13-21. Romans 14:7 states: *For none of us liveth to himself, and no man dieth to himself.* This means that my life affects or **influences others for good or for bad**. What changes do I need to make in my life so that the things I do have a positive influence in my life and the life of others?

4. **Is this thing or activity a negative influence in my life or the life of others?** Is it a habit that is dominating my life? Is it something that is controlling me? In the second part of 1ˢᵗ Corinthians 6:12 the Apostle Paul talks about good things that are not classified as bad: *all things are lawful for me, but I will not be brought under the power of any.* The time that I spend in my work, family activities and relaxation are all important, but it is necessary to do those good things with moderation. Am I being lead and controlled by the Holy Spirit or by other people, possessions and activities?

5. **What would the Lord Jesus Christ do in this activity?** 1ˢᵗ John 2:6 simply declares, *He that saith he abideth in him ought himself also so to walk, even as He walked.* Is my walk or manner of life pleasing to the Lord? Can I give thanks to God in prayer for the activity or thing that I am doing? Is my daily living in obedience to the teaching of the Word of God?

6. **By being involved in this activity, am I being a good testimony for the Lord Jesus Christ?** Am I doing this by faith for the glory of God? The Apostle Paul, in 1ˢᵗ Thessalonians 5:22, gives a solid command telling us to *Abstain from all appearance of evil.* Colossians 3:17 says, *And whatsoever ye do in word or deed, do all in the name of the Lord Jesus, giving thanks to God and the Father by him.* Am I glorifying God with what I do? In 1ˢᵗ Corinthians 10:31, the Apostle Paul challenges us to be careful in everything we do: *Whether therefore ye eat, or drink, or whatsoever ye do, do all to the glory of God.* One must examine his motives carefully to see if his choice is driven by vanity or some other self-centered interest. Can others see Jesus Christ in me? The Apostle Paul gave wise counsel to his co-worker, Timothy, in 1ˢᵗ Timothy 4:12: *Let no man despise thy youth; but be thou an example of the believers, in word, in conversation, in charity, in spirit, in faith, in purity.* Am I a good example of a true Christian?

SUMMARY:

The Christian has daily battles against sin in his life. These conflicts come from the WORLD, the FLESH, and the DEVIL. We have all the resources from God to enable us to have victory in our life. These resources are – (1) Trust in God. (2) Be strengthened in His Word. (3) Watch and pray.

(4) Recognize and confess our sins to receive His forgiveness. (5) Recognize our weaknesses and the great power of God. (6) It is important that we faithfully attend a church where they teach and practice sound biblical doctrines.

God has promised to provide us with a way to escape temptations. We must be submissive to God and resist the devil. We must put on the whole armor of God. We must purpose to be God's instruments of righteousness, separated from the world and its worldly practices. There are six important principal questions that serve as guidelines when the Bible is not clear whether an activity is wrong for us or not. We need to keep these questions in mind to guide us in our decisions.

REVIEW QUESTIONS – CHAPTER 7

POWER TO OVERCOME TEMPTATIONS AND TRIALS

1. What is the only guide for all doctrine and practice in the life of a true Christian? _____

2. 1st John 1:8 was written for believers. Who of us is not capable of sinning? _____

3. Do Christians have spiritual conflicts? _____ Why? _____
   _____

4. What are some characteristics of a life controlled by the new nature of the believer? (Galatians 5:22-23) _____
   _____

5. Name the three principal enemies of all Christians. a. _____
   b. _____ c. _____

6. How does God help us triumph over all temptations that come from the world, the flesh and the devil? (1st Corinthians 10:13) _____
   _____
   _____

122

7. Through what two principal means do we have fellowship with God?
   a. _____   b._____

8. How does the battle in a Christian's life differ from the battles that are fought between two nations? (2nd Corinthians 10:3-5) _____
   _____

9. Why should a Christian be separated from worldliness? (2nd Corinthians 6:14-18; 1st John 2:15-16) _____
   _____
   _____

10. Why does a true Christian need to separate himself from his past religious practices? _____
    _____
    _____

11. What should we do if our thoughts and desires are given to temporal and worldly things? (Philippians 4:8-9; Colossians 3:1-10) _____
    _____
    _____
    _____

12. Which Spirit now dwells in the life of the true Christian? _____
    What verse of Scripture gives us this assurance? _____
    _____
    _____

13. Name briefly six principle guidelines for the Christian regarding questionable activities.

    a. _____

    b. _____

    c. _____

    d. _____

    e. _____

    f. _____

14. Please memorize 1st Corinthians 10:13 and express it in your own words. _____

_____

_____

How can we receive strength to grow in our spiritual life? It is necessary to read and meditate daily in the Word of God so that we enjoy spiritual good health. Please notice how the following lesson gives emphasis to the reading of the Word of God.

Chapter Eight

The Importance of Bible Study

All Scripture is given by inspiration of God, and is profitable for doctrine, for reproof, for correction, for instruction in righteousness: That the man of God may be perfect, thoroughly furnished unto all good works.

2nd Timothy 3:16-17

WHY MUST WE STUDY THE WORD OF GOD?

God's Word is absolute truth, regardless of man's opinions or personal interpretations.

The Bible is a letter given to man by the Spirit of God. The Bible tells us what we need to know, for this reason we need to read it with attentiveness. The Bible teaches us all that is known about God and His plan for our life. It gives us the reason for our existence. It is the only authority over our life, and we should be in subjection to it in all doctrine and practice. God speaks to us through His Word showing His love to us.

125

Many have doubts regarding the Bible, believing that it contains fables and errors. There are people who boast of having read the Bible, but they say that they don't understand it. Some who read the Bible limit their knowledge, reading only some portions of the Old and New Testaments that please them, or they study certain subjects, which are important to them. Studying the Bible in this way brings incomplete and uncertain conclusions. It is important to study the **whole Bible** and learn to use it.

Many Christians know very little about what the Bible says and teaches. It is our desire to help you to understand and appreciate the Bible. The Apostle Paul affirmed in 1st Thessalonians 2:13, *For this cause also thank we God without ceasing, because, when ye received the word of God which ye heard of us, ye received it not as the word of men, but as it is in truth, the _____ of God, which effectually worketh also in you that believe.*

I. THE DIVINE INSPIRATION OF THE BIBLE

1. God is the Author of the Bible.

   The Author of the Bible is God, the Holy Spirit. The only true and living God used and directed at least thirty-nine men, from shepherds to kings, with different abilities and education to write each book using the words that God wanted them to write. They lived in distinct times and places during a period of approximately 1,500 years. With all this, there is unity and harmony in all of its parts. The Holy Scriptures were finalized toward the end of the first century when the Apostle John wrote the book of Revelation. Since then, many have tried to give importance to dreams, visions or other "special messages" from men of fame. **The Bible is the only verbally inspired voice of God given to man,** as we read in 2nd Timothy 3:16-17: *All Scripture is given by inspiration of God, and is _____ for doctrine, for reproof, for correction, for instruction* in righteousness. *That the man of God may be perfect, thoroughly furnished unto all good works.* The Apostle Peter confirms the same truth in 2nd Peter 1:20-21: *Knowing this first, that no prophecy of the Scripture is of any private* [personal] *interpretation. For the prophecy came _____ in old time by the will of man: but holy men of God spake as they were _____* [inspired] *by the Holy Ghost.* In Hebrews 1:1-2, the Apostle Paul also confirmed this: *God, . . . hath in these last days _____ unto us by His Son.*

126

Jesus Christ is 100% man and at the same time 100% God; therefore, when He spoke, it was God speaking. Years later the Holy Spirit inspired the four Evangelist to write the words and events in the life of Jesus Christ in the four Gospels. The apostles wrote many letters under the inspiration of the Holy Spirit, which comprised the rest of the New Testament.

The Apostle Paul, in 1st Corinthians 2:12-13, explained how God gives us comprehension and understanding of the Word of God: *Now we have received, not the spirit of the world, but the spirit which is of God; that we might know the things that are freely given to us of God. Which things also we speak, not in the words which man's wisdom teacheth, but which the Holy Ghost _____; comparing spiritual things with spiritual.* When it says "comparing spiritual things with spiritual," it is teaching the importance of comparing one passage of Scripture with another. This gives us more information regarding the passage, so that it would be more fully understood. He continues explaining in verse 14: *But the natural man receiveth not the things of the Spirit of God: for they are foolishness unto him: neither can he _____ them, because they are spiritually discerned.*

2. The Word of God has power to produce changes in our life.

The Word of God is supernaturally performing its work in the true Christian. Ephesians 1:19 exclaims, *And what is the exceeding greatness of his _____ to us-ward who believe, according to the working of his mighty power!* The word, **working** has reference to "work effectively, efficiently and productively on a supernatural level as energized by God." This is what the Word of God does in the believer. God uses His Word to bring about the conviction of sin, repentance and faith.

In 1st Thessalonians 1:5, the Apostle Paul explained how the Word of God came to us: *For our Gospel came not unto you in word only, but also in _____, and in the Holy Ghost, and in much assurance; as ye know what manner of men we were among you for your sake.* God fortifies and encourages us through His Word. Ephesians 6:10 says, *Finally, my brethren, be strong in the Lord, and in the _____ of His might.* Ephesians 3:20-21 also states, *Now unto him that is able to do exceeding abundantly above all that we ask or think, according to the _____ that worketh in us, unto Him be glory in the church by Christ Jesus throughout all ages, world without end. Amen.*

3. All the Bible is true.

Jesus Christ said in John 18:37, *To this end was I born, and for this cause came I into the world, that I should bear witness unto the* _____. *Every one that is of the truth heareth my voice.* Jesus gave testimony that the **Bible is true**. He also declared it in John 8:47: *He that is of God heareth God's Words.* Psalm 119:160 declares, *Thy word is* _____ *from the beginning: and every one of thy righteous judgments endureth forever.* Jesus Christ prayed in John 17:17: *Sanctify them through thy truth: **thy word is truth**.* The psalmist may have well summarized it all in the magnificent words of Psalm 19:7-11: *The law of the Lord is* _____, *converting the soul: the testimony of the Lord is sure, making wise the simple. The statutes of the Lord are right, rejoicing the heart: the commandment of the Lord is pure, enlightening the eyes. The fear of the Lord is clean, enduring forever: the judgments of the Lord are **true** and righteous altogether. More to be desired are they than gold, yea, than much fine gold: sweeter also than honey and the honeycomb. Moreover, by them is thy servant warned: and in keeping of them there is great reward.*

II. THE CONTENT OF THE BIBLE

The Bible, being verbally inspired by God, is perfect and without error in its content. It is a library of 66 books, which is divided into two parts, the Old and New Testaments. Each book is divided into chapters and each chapter into verses. These divisions are not inspired by God, but have been added to help locate passages much easier. The major part of the Old Testament was written in Hebrew. The major part of the New Testament was written in Greek. The Bible contains the physical and spiritual history of sinful man from the beginning of time. It speaks in general and also in a specific way regarding God's dealings with the chosen nation of Israel, and reveals His Divine plan for all mankind. In the Bible are found all of the doctrines that establish the faith and practice of the church of Jesus Christ. The Word of God is our spiritual food, our guide, our protection from sin, and it stimulates our spiritual growth. The Bible is a love letter from God to us. The paper on which the Bible is written is not holy; however, its content is sacred.

The principal person of the Bible is the Lord Jesus Christ, the only God and Savior of the world. The Old Testament points forward to our Lord Jesus Christ and the New Testament points back to our Lord Jesus Christ.

Old Testament ☞ **Jesus Christ** ☜ New Testament

God's Word revealed in Psalm 19

1. What are the six **names** that David used when He referred to God's Word in Psalm 19?

    (1) 19:7 _____

    (2) 19:7 _____

    (3) 19:8 _____

    (4) 19:8 _____

    (5) 19:9 _____

    (6) 19:9 _____

2. What are the six **characteristics** (a quality) of God's Word referred to in Psalm 19?

    (1) 19:7 It is like: _____

    (2) 19:7 It is like: _____

    (3) 19:8 It is like: _____

    (4) 19:8 It is like: _____

    (5) 19:9 It is like: _____

    (6) 19:9 It is like: _____

3. How does the Word of God **benefit us**?

    (1) 19:7 _____

    (2) 19:7 _____

    (3) 19:8 _____

    (4) 19:8 _____

    (5) 19:9 _____

III. THE DIVISIONS OF THE BIBLE.

1. THE OLD TESTAMENT contains 39 books.

    a. The Law or the Pentateuch (5 books of Moses)

    b. The History of Israel (12 books)

    c. The Poetry (5 books)

    d. The Major Prophets (5 books)

    e. The Minor Prophets (12 books)

(The last book of the Old Testament was written 400 years before the birth of Jesus Christ.)

2. THE NEW TESTAMENT contains 27 books.

(All these books were written after the birth of Jesus Christ.)

    a. The History of the Life of Jesus Christ (the 4 Gospels)

    b. The History of the Primitive Church (1 book)

    c. The Church Doctrine (21 letters to churches and individuals)

    d. The Prophecy – Revelation (1 book)

(Besides the book of Revelation, there are many prophecies throughout the entire Bible.)

- **IMPORTANT HOMEWORK:**

You should memorize the names of the books of the Bible in their correct order. In this way you will be able to locate the different books of the Bible with ease. I recommend that you first memorize the names of the books of the New Testament and then those of the Old Testament.

IV. HOW CAN WE RECEIVE THE GREATEST BENEFIT FROM THE BIBLE?

1. We need to **hear** the Word of God.

    If we want to grow in our Christian life, it is important to hear God's Word by faithfully attending Sunday School, church services and Bible studies. It is also advantageous to listen to good Christian programs on the radio or on the Internet, if they are of sound doctrine. I enjoy and recommend listening daily to the reading of God's Word, using cassettes, CD's or iPods. In Romans 10:17, the Apostle Paul tells us how we receive the faith of God: *So then faith cometh by hearing, and hearing by the _____ of God.* Why is it important to listen to the teaching and preaching of the Word of God? _____

    _____

2. We need to **read** the Word of God.

    We have to take time to read God's Word, put it into practice and live in obedience to what God is teaching. As we dedicate time to our personal reading, the Bible has the power to transform our lives. An effective method is to have a daily plan for reading the Word of God and to have fellowship with God through prayer. I recommend that you read at least three chapters from a specific book of the Bible each day. I suggest that you start with the Gospel of Mark or John, after this read the letter to the Romans, and then continue with a plan to finish reading the entire Bible. Hebrews 4:12 expresses what the Word of God does in our life: *For the Word of God is quick* [alive], *and powerful, and sharper than any two-edged sword, piercing even to the dividing asunder of soul and spirit, and of the joints and marrow, and is a _____ of the thoughts and intents of the heart.*

3. We need to **study** the Word of God.

    The Word of God is the only guide and true authority in which we can fully trust. The command given in 2nd Timothy 2:15 is important: *Study to shew thyself approved unto God, a workman that needeth not to be ashamed, _____ dividing* [interpreting] *the word of truth.* In order to be grounded in the Word of God and grow spiritually, it is important to attend the Bible studies and the worship services of your church. 1st Peter 2:2 tells us, *As newborn babes, _____ the sincere milk of the Word, that ye may grow thereby.* Colossians 3:16

131

explains what God wants us to do: *Let the word of Christ* _____ *in you richly in all wisdom; teaching and admonishing one another in psalms and hymns and spiritual songs, singing with grace in your hearts to the Lord.* I recommend the use of other books and Bible commentaries for additional study. The pastor of your church can recommend some Bible study books and correspondence courses so that you can continue studying at home. If you do not have a pastor, you can write to me for additional information and I will be happy to provide a list of Bible study books that will be of help.

In 2nd Timothy 3:16-17, several ways are mentioned as to how God uses His Word in our life.

a. It is profitable for _____, (correct biblical teaching)

b. It is profitable for _____, (to examine our very being for the purpose of pointing out our errors and the sin in our life.)

c. It is profitable for _____, (to discipline us, to bring repentance and to correct our wrong way of living.)

d. It is profitable for _____ in righteousness (to guide us in right living)

e. It is profitable for _____, (maturing)

2nd Tim. 3:16 teaches – *All scripture is given by inspiration of God, and is profitable for doctrine* = **"To teach you what is right.**
for reproof = **To show you what is not right.**
for correction = **To show you how to get right.**
for instruction in righteousness = **To teach you how to stay right." (Wiersbe)**

God wants to prepare us day by day so that we can be spiritually mature persons and ready to serve Him better.

4. We need to **meditate** on the Word of God.

As our daily food is important for our body, so is the Word of God for our soul and spirit. Joshua 1:8 helps us to appreciate the importance to meditate in God's Word: *This book of the law shall not depart out of thy mouth; but thou shalt **meditate** therein day and night, that thou mayest* _____ *to do according to all that is written therein:*

132

for then thou shalt make thy way prosperous, and then thou shalt have good success. When reading a portion of God's Word, take time to meditate on it, and think about how to apply it to your life; afterwards, put in to practice what you have learned. We read in Ezra 7:10, *For Ezra had _____ his heart to seek the law of the Lord, and to do it, and to teach in Israel statutes and judgments.* Psalm 1:2 shows the desires of the heart of the believer: *But his delight is in the law of the Lord; and in his law doth he _____ day and night.* Isaiah 26:3 declares, *Thou wilt keep him in perfect peace, whose mind is stayed* [meditating] *on thee: because he _____ in thee.*

5. We need to **memorize** the Word of God.

    By memorizing Bible verses we are spiritually strengthened and our thoughts are steadfast in His Word to help us in times of testing. We read in Psalm 119:11, *Thy Word have I hid in mine heart, that I might not _____ against thee.* Only through memorizing God's Word can we maintain stability in our life. A good goal is to memorize one Scripture verse each week. This will have a significant impact on your life and will help you to grow spiritually.

    When we memorize Bible verses we are preparing ourselves for opportunities to share God's Word in the future. The Apostle Peter taught in 1st Peter 3:15, *Be ready always to give an _____ to every man that asketh you a reason of the hope that is in you with meekness and fear.* Memorizing the Word of God is the best way to be prepared to testify to others. Through memorization, the Word of God becomes part of our very being.

6. We need to **obey** the Word of God.

    It is essential that we put into practice the teachings that we receive from the Bible. In Romans 16:19, the Apostle Paul expressed his gratitude for the obedience of the brethren: *For your _____ is come abroad unto all men. I am glad therefore on your behalf: but yet I would have you wise unto that which is good, and simple* [lack of experience] *concerning evil.* In Luke 11:28, Jesus Christ declared, *Yea rather,* [more] *blessed are they that hear the word of God, and keep it* [obey it]. In order *to grow in grace and the knowledge of the Lord Jesus Christ* it is important to give attention to what is taught in 1st Peter 1:14-16: *As obedient children, not fashioning yourselves according to the former lusts in your ignorance: But as he which hath called you is holy, so be ye _____ in all manner of conversation* [manner of living]*; Because it is written, Be ye holy; for I am holy.* The Christian lives by biblical principles and not by rules and laws, for sin changes its form continually, but principles do not. We should never violate biblical principles when we are asked to do things that are incorrect. Our response to them should always be the same as that of the apostles in Acts 5:27-**29**: *We ought to _____ **God** rather than men.* Now that we belong to Jesus Christ, our sincere desire is to obey Him and be governed by His Word.

7. We need to **teach** the Word of God to others.

To be able to teach the Word of God correctly to others we have to prepare ourselves. The Apostle Paul admonished us in 2nd Timothy 2:2, *The things that thou hast heard of me among many witnesses, the same commit thou to faithful men, who shall be able to _____ others also.* When Jesus chose His apostles in Matthew 4:19, He commanded them, *Follow me, and I will make you fishers of men.* After Jesus Christ had taught His apostles, He sent them out two by two to proclaim the Gospel. They were well equipped with His teachings. Jesus gave to all of us the great commission in Mark 16:15: *Go ye into all the world, and preach the _____ to every creature.* In Matthew 28:19-20, Jesus Christ commands His disciples saying, *Go ye therefore, and _____ all nations, baptizing them in the name of the Father, and of the Son, and of the Holy Spirit.* This command of Christ applies to all Christians! We have to share His glorious message with the world around us.

SUMMARY:

The Bible is inspired by the Holy Spirit of God and is composed of 66 books, which are divided into the Old and the New Testaments. The principal person of the Bible is the Lord Jesus Christ, the only God and Savior of the world. Throughout the Bible the physical and spiritual history of sinful man is presented. The Bible is spiritual food, a guide and a protection from sin. It stimulates our spiritual growth. To be beneficial to us, we have to hear the Word of God, read it, study it, memorize it and meditate upon it. By doing all this, the final results should be our obedience with all our heart to the teachings of God's Word. Throughout the Word of God, the Holy Spirit not only teaches us doctrine, but also, how to think, to live and to act. We cannot permit ourselves to be deceived by error. God's Word teaches us that we must reject visions, dreams and other spectacular manifestations.

We have the whole Word of God written in its final and complete form in the Bible. One can read the whole Bible in 80 hours! I suggest you read at least three chapters of the Bible every day and meditate upon it. If you read three chapters every day and five on Sunday, you will be able to read the Bible through in one year. I encourage you to memorize each key text given at the beginning of each chapter of this book. Also, I encourage you to memorize other verses and important chapters of the Bible. Philippians 2:13 tells us that God will help us to do what is right: *For it is God which worketh in you both to will and to* _____ *of his good pleasure.*

REVIEW QUESTIONS – CHAPTER 8

THE IMPORTANCE OF BIBLE STUDY

1. The only true Author of the Bible is God, the _____ _____

2. Approximately how many men did God use to write the Bible? _____

3. Who is the principle Person of the Bible? _____

4. (True) or (False) The Bible was verbally inspired by God.

5. (True) or (False) Only part of the Bible was verbally inspired by God.

6. (True) or (False) There are no errors in the original manuscripts of the Bible.

7. (True) or (False) The paper and ink with which the Bible was written is sacred.

8. The Old Testament points forward to _____ and the New Testament points back to _____.

9. The major divisions of the Old Testament are:

    a. The _____ or the _____ (5 Books)

    b. The _____ of Israel (12 books)

    c. The _____ (5 books)

    d. The _____ _____ (5 books)

    e. The _____ _____ (12 books)

135

10. The major divisions of the New Testament are:

    a.   The history of the life of _____ _____ (4 Gospels)

    b.   The history of the _____ _____ (1 Book)

    c.   The _____ _____ (21 letters)

    d.   The _____ or Revelation (1 book)

11. In 2nd Timothy 3:16-17 what five ways does God use His Word in our life?

    a.   It is profitable for _____, (teaching)

    b.   It is profitable for _____, (investigation for the purpose of showing us where we are wrong)

    c.   It is profitable for _____, (discipline)

    d.   It is profitable for _____ in righteousness:

    e.   It is profitable for _____, (maturing)

12. What must we do to take advantage of God's teaching?

    a.   _____ the Word of God.

    b.   _____ the Word of God.

    c.   _____ the Word of God.

    d.   _____ the Word of God.

    e.   _____ the Word of God.

    f.   _____ the Word of God.

    g.   _____ the Word of God to others.

13. Please memorize 2nd Timothy 3:16-17 and express it in your own words.

_____

_____

_____

One of the most effective methods to have communion with God is to daily dedicate a special time in the morning to read the Bible and pray. The following lesson shows the importance of having time together with God in prayer.

Chapter Nine

The Importance of Prayer

*For we have not an high priest which cannot be touched
with the feeling of our infirmities; but was in all points
tempted like as we are, yet without sin. Let us therefore come boldly
unto the throne of grace, that we may obtain mercy,
and find grace to help in time of need.*
Hebrews 4:15-16

GOD DESIRES OUR FELLOWSHIP WITH HIM.

Prayer is one part of our intimate fellowship with God. With confidence and a contrite and humble heart, we should make time to be alone with God. Prayer is directed to God and is an expression of the most intimate thoughts of our heart. It is a privilege to be able to speak directly with God, our Father, through our Savior, the Lord Jesus Christ. If we love Him, we will want to spend time with Him daily. God has shown His love to us, so we should respond to that love. The best form of expressing real love is by seeking opportunities to be with the one we love. It is amazing and humbling for us to know that God loves us and wants to have communion with us.

I. WHY SHOULD WE PRAY?

1. We pray because it is a privilege and at the same time a solemn responsibility. Our key verse for this lesson, Hebrews 4:15-16, gives us an invitation to come boldly before God. What a privilege! Prayer is necessary in order to receive His mercy, grace and help. God said in 2nd Chronicles 7:14-15, *If my people, which are called by my name, shall humble themselves, and _____, and seek my face, and turn from their wicked ways; then will **I hear from Heaven**, and will forgive their sin, and will heal their land. Now mine eyes shall be open, and **mine ears attent unto the prayer** that is made in this place.* God really hears the prayers of those who belong to Him! Philippians 4:6-7 *Be careful for nothing; but in every thing by prayer and supplication with thanksgiving let your requests be made known unto God. And the peace of God, which passeth all understanding, shall keep your hearts and minds through Christ Jesus.*

2. We pray because it is an example given by Jesus Christ, the apostles and the early church. Jesus Christ set aside time to talk to His Heavenly Father. Mark 1:35 states, *And in the morning, rising up a great while before day, he went out, and departed into a solitary place, and there prayed.* Luke 6:12 shows the importance He gave to prayer: *And it came to pass in those days, that he went out into a mountain to _____, and continued all night in prayer to God.* Likewise, we need to spend much more time in prayer!

    Great importance was given to prayer by the early church. The apostles had been overwhelmed with outside distractions, preventing them from spending time in the Word of God and prayer. In Acts 6:2, the apostles presented a distressing problem to the brethren: *It is not reason that we should leave the word of God, and serve tables.* The correct solution to this need was presented in Acts 6:3-4: *Wherefore, brethren, look [search] ye out among you seven men of honest report, full of the Holy Spirit and wisdom, whom we may appoint over this business. But we will give ourselves continually to _____, and to the ministry of the Word.*

3. The tendency to forget our need to pray opens the door to temptation, which can result in sin. Many times the activities of the day and the urgencies of work distract our attention from this important fellowship with God. In Matthew 26:41, Jesus said to the apostles,

Watch and pray, that ye enter not into _____: *the spirit indeed is willing, but the flesh is* **weak**. We are weak and we need to rely on a time of prayer with the Lord Jesus Christ, as James 4:7 teaches: *Submit yourselves therefore to God. Resist the devil, and he will flee from you.* In 1st Corinthians 10:12, the Apostle Paul admonishes every Christian as to the danger of thinking that we are self-sufficient and capable of resisting sin and temptation in our own power: *Wherefore let him that thinketh he standeth take* _____ *lest he fall.* It is important to set aside a certain time and place to have this fellowship with Him.

II. WHO CAN PRAY?

1. The repentant sinner can pray. The thief on the cross, pled for mercy and God saved him. God also wants to hear your prayers. King David poured out his heart to God in Psalm 51:15-17: *O Lord, open thou my lips; and my mouth shall shew forth thy praise. For thou desirest not sacrifice; else would I give it: thou delightest not in burnt offering. The sacrifices of God are a broken spirit: a broken and a contrite* _____, *O God, thou wilt not despise.* When God hears our repentant and humble prayers, He shows us mercy.

   The convincing story of Cornelius, described in Acts 10:1-48, shows how Cornelius prayed to God with all sincerity. God heard and answered him by sending the Apostle Peter to share the Gospel with him. Cornelius and his family heard, believed and were saved. Their lives were changed forever.

2. It is important to teach your children to pray and not just have them repeat empty words. In 1st Samuel 3:10, we read about Samuel, who as a small child trusted in God and spoke directly with Him: *And the Lord came, and stood, and called as at other times, Samuel, Samuel. Then Samuel answered, Speak; for thy servant* _____. He truly understood that God was talking to him. Children are important to God and He sees their tenderness, simplicity and faith. In Matthew 19:14, Jesus showed His appreciation for the children: *But Jesus said, Suffer* [permit] *little children, and forbid them not, to come unto me: for of such is the kingdom of Heaven.* It is our great responsibility to train our children to trust in God and seek Him at an early age, as stated in Proverbs.

3. All those who have truly placed their faith in the Lord Jesus Christ as their personal Savior have the right to pray. The Word of God declares in 1st Peter 3:12: *For the eyes of the Lord are over the righteous* [those who have been saved through Jesus Christ], *and His ears are open unto their _____: but the face of the Lord is against them that do evil.* Hebrews 4:15-16 shows that we have a Great High Priest (Jesus Christ), who is compassionate, hears our prayers and intercedes for us before God.

III. UNDER WHAT CONDITIONS DOES GOD ANSWER PRAYER?

God gives conditions for our prayers to be answered.

1. God requires **holiness** in our daily living. He desires that our lives be clean. God wants to forgive and cleanse us from our sins according to 1st John 1:9: *If we confess our sins, he is faithful and just to forgive us our sins, and to _____ us from all unrighteousness.* Our tendency is to attempt to justify our sin, but the Bible tells us to come to Him with a repentant and contrite heart. We have to recognize and confess our sins, which are offences against God. What will be the results? The Lord Jesus Christ is faithful and just to forgive and cleanse us of all our sins.

2. In 2nd Corinthians 7:1, the Apostle Paul instructs all believers to **clean up** their lives from all contamination of the flesh, heart and the mind: *Having therefore these promises, dearly beloved, let us _____ ourselves from all filthiness of the flesh and spirit, perfecting holiness in the fear of God.* We must cleanse ourselves from those things and influences that cause us to drift away from a holy life. God demands that we cleanse our lives from those things that affect our spirit and damage our relationship, fellowship and harmony with Him.

3. Psalm 37:4 explains that **obedience** on our part is a condition to have our prayers answered: *Delight thyself also in the Lord: and he shall give thee the desires of thine heart.* It is crucial that we search His Word for the purpose of obeying it joyfully. We must obey God's Word as stated in 1st John 3:22: *Whatsoever we ask, we receive of Him, because we keep* [obey] *His commandments* [His instructions], *and _____ those things that are pleasing in His sight.*

4. God places **faithfulness** to Him and His Word as a priority for having

our prayers answered. In John 15:7, the Lord Jesus Christ said, *If ye _____ in me, and my words abide in you, ye shall ask what you will, and it shall be done unto you.* This shows us the importance of abiding in Him so that we will know what to ask according to His will. We must faithfully follow Him as mentioned in John 10:27: *My sheep hear my voice, and I know them, **and they follow me**.* We must faithfully study His Word daily, so that His Word can live in us. **God never rewards unfaithfulness.**

5. God commands us to pray **according to His will**, not according to what we desire. Israel stubbornly insisted on doing their own will, but notice the remarks of the psalmist in Psalm 106:15: *And he gave them their request; but sent _____ into their soul.* The Apostle John teaches us, in 1st John 5:14-15, a very important truth about asking for the correct things: *This is the confidence that we have in him, that, if we ask any thing according to _____ will, He heareth us: And if we know that he hear us, whatsoever we ask, we know that we have the petitions that we desired of him.* It is important for us to pray according to the teachings of God's Word. In this way, we know our requests will be in agreement with the will of God, and not just according to what we think we need. When He does not give us what we request, we should recognize that He knows what is best for us. We need to ask God for wisdom, so that we can please Him, even in our requests. James 1:5 says, *If any of you lack wisdom, **let him _____ of God,** that giveth to all men liberally, and upbraideth not; and it shall be given him.* The more we read God's Word, the more we understand His will.

Prayer is not a mystical exercise that Christians use to twist the arm of God, obligating Him to answer their petitions. Neither is it a physiological exercise to make us feel good. We should not think by depriving ourselves of food (by fasting) will obligate God to give us what we want. We cannot negotiate with God in order to receive our petitions. It is important for us to have the same attitude of Jesus Christ as expressed in Luke 22:42: *not my will, but thine, be done.* The answer to the Apostle Paul's prayer, in 2nd Corinthians 12:8-9, was, "No!" God answered him by saying, *My grace is sufficient for thee: for my strength is made perfect in weakness.* Sometimes we receive a negative answer, because we have asked for the wrong things. James 4:3 confirms this fact: *Ye ask, and receive not, because ye ask* _____ , *that ye may consume it upon your lusts.* Even though God knows beforehand what we need, He still wants to hear our prayers. God always answers our prayers. Sometimes His answer is "Yes," and sometimes His answer is "No." On other occasions God tells us to "Wait," because it is not the opportune time to give us what we are requesting. We must always remember that God is good and He never makes a mistake. He is Sovereign!

IV. WHERE SHOULD WE PRAY?

God desires that we pray to Him wherever we are and at any time. The apostles prayed everywhere and in all circumstances, and we should have the same practice. In 1st Timothy 2:8, the Apostle Paul expresses this desire: *I will therefore that men pray everywhere.* We can talk with God in prayer and be in an attitude of fellowship with Him, no matter what the circumstances are that surround us. Many interpret wrongly the last part of 1st Timothy 2:8: ***lifting up holy hands**, without wrath and doubting.* **This has nothing to do with our physical hands,** but only has reference in a symbolic manner to help us realize that God sees the sin that we have committed and the guilt we have on our hands. God insists that we recognize the sin in our life, repent and confess it to Him. This is the only way that God can see our **"holy hands"** as we daily strive to live holy lives. All unconfessed sin affects our life, and it affects others.

V. WHEN CAN WE PRAY?

1st Thessalonians 5:17 affirms, *Pray without ceasing.* We should always be in an attitude conducive to prayer, having the confidence that God is present and hears us. It is important to be in intimate fellowship with God whenever and wherever we may be. We should pray in moments of need and also of joy. King David expressed this in Psalm 55:17: *Evening and morning, and at noon, will I* _____ *and cry aloud: and He shall hear my voice.* Praying should be as natural as breathing. Ephesians 6:18 says, *Praying **always** with all prayer and supplication in the Spirit, and watching thereunto with all perseverance and supplication for all saints.* The use of the word, "saint" here has reference to all of us who belong to God.

VI. HOW SHOULD WE PRAY?

Having observed Jesus Christ pray many times, the apostles saw the emphasis that He placed upon prayer. They understood that prayer was not a mere repetition of words. In Luke 11:1, one of His disciples

142

requested that He teach them to pray: *And it came to pass, that, as he was praying in a certain place, when he ceased, one of his disciples said unto him, Lord, _____ us to pray, as John also taught his disciples.* The Lord Jesus Christ gave them a model for prayer in Matthew 6:9-13 that is brief, simple and understood. He did not give them this prayer to memorize in order to be recited as a prayer, but as a guide. He taught them in Matthew 6:9: *After this manner therefore pray ye.* He said, "after this manner," **not with these words.**

1. We should go to God with reverence and worship. We should give Him all honor and adoration, not only with our mind and mouth, but also with our life. God is Sovereign, Omnipotent (All-powerful), Omniscient (All-knowing), Omnipresent (All-present), Eternal, King of Kings and Lord of Lords. The Apostle Paul let words of adoration flow from his heart in 1st Timothy 6:15-16: *Which in his times he shall show, who is the blessed and only Potentate, the King of kings, and Lord of Lords; Who only hath immortality, dwelling in the light which no man can approach unto; whom no man hath seen, nor can see: to whom be honor and power everlasting. Amen.* Many of the Psalms are prayers of praise and adoration to God. An example is Psalm 104:1, *Bless the Lord, O my soul, O Lord my God, thou art very great; thou art clothed with honor and majesty.* Other good examples of praise are Psalm 29:2; Psalm 34:3; and Isaiah 25:1.

   Many make the mistake of referring to God with such refrains as "the man upstairs," etc. Never should we use such expressions in reference to God, for it is a great lack of respect and blasphemy! Listen to the advice given in Ecclesiastes 5:2: *Be not rash with thy mouth, and let not thine heart be hasty to utter anything before God: for God is in Heaven, and thou upon earth: therefore **let thy words be few.*** Our prayers should not be frivolous, self-centered or irresponsible. It is wrong to speak with absurdities, and not think about what we say.

2. We should approach God with the intention of receiving cleansing from our sin. James 4:8-10 shows the necessity for us to be cleansed: *Draw nigh to God, and he will draw nigh to you. _____ your hands, ye sinners; and purify your hearts, ye double minded. Be afflicted, and mourn, and weep: let your laughter be turned to mourning, and your joy to heaviness. Humble yourselves in the sight of the Lord, and he shall lift you up.* It is necessary to go to God with repentance, confess our sins and ask Jesus Christ for forgiveness

so that God will hear us. Is it possible that God will not hear your prayer? Psalm 66:18 warns, *If I regard iniquity* [sin] *in my heart, the Lord will _____ hear me.* The confession of sin in prayer each day is vital to maintain our fellowship and a good relationship with God. What promise does God make when we confess our sins to Him and forsake them? Proverbs 28:13 declares, *He that covereth his sins shall not prosper: but whoso _____ and _____ them shall have mercy.* Jesus Christ requires that we go to Him and confess our sins to receive His pardon and cleansing. Unconfessed sin has many bad effects on our physical and spiritual life. It is also a bad testimony to the unsaved around us, and gives them reason to reject the message of the Gospel.

3. We should express our gratitude to God for everything that He has done in our life, and for the daily provisions that we receive. In Colossians 4:2, the Apostle Paul admonishes us, *Continue in prayer, and watch in the same with _____.* In 1st Corinthians 15:57, he gives thanks to God for victories in his life: *But thanks be to God, which giveth us the victory through our Lord Jesus Christ.* Also, in Ephesians 5:20, the Apostle Paul reminds us to always give thanks for everything: *Giving thanks always for all things unto God and the Father, in the name of our Lord Jesus Christ.* Colossians 3:17 teaches us to express gratitude for all that the Lord is permitting us to do: *And whatsoever ye do in word or deed, do all in the name of the Lord Jesus, giving thanks to God and the Father by him.*

We should express our gratitude to the Lord for His grace to us. *Grace* is the "outpouring of God's unsolicited and undeserved goodness" upon sinful men. This goodness, however, may not always be recognized, for sometimes it comes in the form of pain and suffering. We should remember that God shows His goodness as He deals with mankind in general, and with us in particular. Whatever comes into our life has come from the God of all grace, who has purposed to enrich our life by His gift, whether it be in what He gives, or what He takes away. It is a holy privilege to be able to go to God, enjoy fellowship together and talk to Him about our joys and sorrows. The expressions of King David in the Psalms many times are expressions of the deeper feelings of his heart. Psalm 31:19 exclaims, *Oh how great is Thy goodness, which thou hast laid up for them that fear thee; which thou hast wrought for them that trust in thee before the sons of men!* When we think of God's kindness, of His grace, of His love and of His mercy, how can we help but express our gratitude to Him!

4. We should recognize that the Holy Spirit continually helps us in prayer. Many times we do not know what we should ask for, or how to ask for it. The Apostle Paul teaches this truth in Romans 8:26: *Likewise the Spirit also helpeth our infirmities* [natural human weaknesses]: *for we know ____ what we should pray for as we ought: but the _____ itself maketh intercession for us with groanings which cannot be uttered.* This passage indicates that sometimes our petitions cannot be easily expressed. The Holy Spirit, knowing our heart and our needs, intercedes for us. He will communicate correctly our petition to the Father. Besides this, the Spirit of God makes requests for us according to the perfect will of God. It affirms this in Romans 8:27, *And He that searcheth the hearts knoweth what is the mind of the Spirit, because He maketh intercession for the saints according to the _____ of God.* What a comfort!

5. We are always in the presence of God; therefore, we lift our hearts to the "throne of grace" through our Lord Jesus Christ. His "name" corresponds to His character and all that He represents. According to John 15:16, what are four conditions for having our prayers answered? Jesus said, *Ye have not chosen me, but I have chosen you, and ordained you, that ye should go and bring forth fruit, and that your fruit should remain: that whatsoever ye shall ask of the Father in my name, He may give it you.* 1. You have been _____. 2. You should go and bring forth _____. 3. Your fruit should _____. 4. Ask the Father in the name of _____.

6. We should pray with faith. Prayer must be offered with confident trust in a Sovereign God without doubting. James 1:6 instructs, *But let him ask in faith, nothing _____. For he that wavereth is like a wave of the sea driven with the wind and tossed.* Instead of being worried or frustrated because of our problems and needs, what should we do? The Apostle Paul teaches us in Philippians 4:6, *But in everything by prayer and supplication with thanksgiving let your requests be made _____ unto God.*

7. We must pray with sincerity. Many pray because it is custom or practice, but God gives instructions in Hebrews 10:21-22: *And having an high priest* [Jesus Christ] *over the house of God; Let us draw near with a true* [sincere] *heart in full assurance of faith, having*

our hearts sprinkled from an evil conscience, and our bodies washed with pure water [the Word of God]. God saw into the future of Israel and revealed it in Jeremiah 29:11-13: *For I _____ the thoughts that I think toward you, saith the Lord, thoughts of peace, and not of evil, to give you an expected end. Then shall ye call upon me, and ye shall go and pray unto me, and I will hearken unto you. And ye shall seek me, and find me, when ye shall search for me with all your _____.* Seeing the sincerity of Jeremiah, God gave him the answers to his prayers. We must express our own feelings and thoughts from the depth of our very being. We do not use a "prayer book."

8. God rejects vain repetitions when we pray. Our prayers should not be just empty words that have been memorized. Matthew 6:7-8 teaches us that we should not use memorized prayers or empty repetition in our prayer: *But when ye pray, **use not vain repetitions**, as the heathen do: for they think that they shall be heard for their much speaking. Be not ye therefore like unto them: for your Father knoweth what things ye have need of, before ye ask him.* Another example of the use of vain repetitions is to say, "Oh, Lord Jesus" or "Oh, God," at the beginning of each sentence or new thought. This is not a normal way of speaking! We would never say to a friend, "Oh, Peter, oh Peter my friend, oh Peter listen." This is not normal.

9. We should always recognize our need to pray. It is our responsibility to be alert and to maintain the communication lines open with the Lord. Recognizing the seriousness of this life, and the fact of the soon return of our Lord and Savior Jesus Christ to earth for us, the Apostle Paul admonished in Hebrews 10:25: *Not forsaking the _____ of ourselves together, as the manner of some is; but exhorting one another: and so much the more, as ye see the _____ approaching.* We need to meet together as the family of God to worship, hear the preaching of God's Word and pray. For this reason 1st Peter 4:7 emphasizes our need to be *sober, and _____ unto prayer.* The word **watch** indicates in this verse **the urgency of being alert** to the dangers that try to derail us from the joy of intimate fellowship with God and the brethren. We have to be serious with ourselves and maintain our time of prayer with Him.

10. We have to maintain order and respect when we pray. It is a joy to be united in prayer with other brethren; however, there should not

be more than one person praying audibly at the same time. While another person is praying, we should be quiet and attentive to the petitions of the one praying, so that we can say, "Amen." ***Amen*** means – "**May it be so**." This shows we are in agreement with the prayer. This teaching is found in 1ˢᵗ Corinthians 14:16: *Else when thou shalt bless with the spirit, how shall he that occupieth the room of the unlearned say _____ at thy giving of thanks.* Acts 1:14 tells us that when the early Christians met to pray they were unanimous: *These all continued with ____ accord in prayer and supplication.* They were **unanimous in spirit and purpose**, but they were not speaking all at the same time. We must maintain order and respect when we pray. God is not the author of confusion, nor does he permit it. The Apostle Paul taught in 1ˢᵗ Corinthians 14:40, *Let all things be done _____ and in order.* There are those who desire to turn prayer into an emotional experience, rather than a time to reverently seek the Lord with their whole heart. All disorder is in direct disobedience to God's Word. Are you obeying and honoring God in the way you pray? God wants you to have order in your life, in the home, in the work place, and in the church.

VII. FOR WHOM SHOULD WE PRAY?

The Bible teaches a great deal regarding the people for whom we should pray. The Bible, in both the Old and New Testaments, gives many examples of God's servants who prayed. We understand that most of their prayers involved intercession for the spiritual needs of the people, far more than for their physical, emotional and material needs.

1. We need to pray for **ourselves**. Jeremiah 33:3 teaches, *Call unto me, and I will _____ thee, and shew thee great and mighty things, which thou knowest not.* God continually blesses us as we continue to call upon Him. In 2ⁿᵈ Timothy 2:22, the Apostle Paul instructed Timothy, *Flee also youthful lusts: but follow righteousness, faith, charity, peace, with them that _____ on the Lord out of a pure heart.* As we continue to pray for ourselves, remember the testimony of the Psalmist in Psalm 73:28: *But it is good for me to draw near to God: I have put my _____ in the Lord God, that I may declare all thy works.* We need to express our love and gratitude to the Lord for what He has done for us. He enriches our life far beyond our comprehension or what we deserve!

2. We need to pray for **others**. We must pray for our family and friends, for believers and for unbelievers. Jesus Christ prayed for unbelievers and even for his enemies who would someday place their trust in Him, repent of their sin and give themselves to Him. Jesus Christ prayed in John 17:20, *Neither pray I for these alone, but for them also which _____ believe on me through their word.* A person can only come to the Lord for salvation by the power and grace of God. We should pray that God would work in the hearts of those who do not know the Lord as their Savior. Do you pray only for your family or do you also have a concern for others? It is important to pray specifically for the salvation of people outside your immediate circle.

3. We need to pray for the **brethren** in the faith. Every true Christian forms part of a great family, the family of God. Our petitions are important to God and we should pray for the spiritual needs of others. The Bible teaches us to pray one for another. In Colossians 1:9-10, the Apostle Paul expressed the great need: *For this cause we also, since the day we heard it, do not cease to pray for _____, and to desire that ye might be filled with the knowledge of His will in all wisdom and spiritual understanding. That ye might walk worthy of the Lord unto all pleasing, being fruitful in every good work, and increasing in the knowledge of God.* In Ephesians 3:14-19, the Apostle Paul prayed with a great concern for the spiritual progress of the brethren: *For this cause I bow my knees unto the Father of our Lord Jesus Christ, . . . that he would grant you, according to the riches of his glory, to be _____ with might by his Spirit in the inner man; that Christ may dwell in your hearts by faith; that ye, being rooted and grounded in love, may be able to comprehend with all saints what is the breadth, and length, and depth, and height; and to know the love of Christ, which passeth knowledge, that ye might be filled with all the fullness of God.*

Again the love and concern of the Apostle Paul is clearly seen in 1st Thessalonians 3:9-10: *For what thanks can we render to God again for you, for all the joy wherewith we joy for your sakes before our God; Night and day _____ exceedingly that we might see your face, and might perfect [complete] that which is lacking in your faith?*

4. We need to pray for those who are **sick**. The Apostle Paul mentioned, in Philippians 2:27, that he prayed especially for Epaphroditus: *For indeed he was sick nigh unto death: but God had _____ on*

148

him; and not on him only, but on me also, lest I should have sorrow upon sorrow. James 5:14-16 asks the question, *Is any sick among you? Let **him** _____ for the elders* [pastors] *of the church; and let them pray over him, anointing him with oil in the name of the Lord: And the prayer of faith shall save* [heal] *the sick, and the Lord shall raise him up; and if he have committed sins, they shall be forgiven him. Confess your faults one to another, and pray one for another, that ye may be healed. The effectual fervent prayer of a righteous man availeth much.* It is important to always pray that the Lord's will be done.

5. It is a great responsibility and privilege to pray for those who are actively serving the Lord in various **ministries**. These servants of God are reaching out to the lost, and helping Christian to grow in their spiritual life. They are pastors, teachers, missionaries, evangelists and others in the ministry. The Apostle Paul requests in 2nd Thessalonians 3:1-2, *Finally, brethren, _____ for us, that the Word of the Lord may have free course, and be glorified, even as it is with you: And that we may be delivered from unreasonable and wicked men: for all men have not faith.* We can help these ministers of God by praying for their spiritual life, for their ministries and for their personal needs. In Ephesians 6:18-20, the Apostle Paul instructed the brethren how they should pray: *Praying always with all prayer and supplication in the Spirit, and watching thereunto with all perseverance and supplication for all **saints**; and for me, that utterance may be given unto me, that I may open my mouth boldly, to make known the mystery of the _____, for which I am an ambassador in bonds: that therein I may speak boldly, as I ought to speak.* He also expressed the need to pray for each other, that we might witness with wisdom and boldness. 2nd Thessalonians 1:11-12 *Wherefore also we pray always for you, that our God would count you worthy of this calling, and fulfil all the good pleasure of his goodness, and the work of faith with power: That the name of our Lord Jesus Christ may be glorified in you, and ye in him, according to the grace of our God and the Lord Jesus Christ.*

6. We should pray for all those who are in **authority** over us. The Apostle Paul commanded in 1st Timothy 2:1-2, *I exhort therefore, that, first of all, supplications, prayers, intercessions, and giving of thanks, be made for all men; for kings, and for all that are in _____; that we may lead a quiet and peaceable life in all godliness and honesty.* Even here the Apostle Paul is including his

concerns for the salvation of the authorities in government. Do not forget to pray that the message of salvation will reach them also.

Summary:

We must communicate with God with confidence, but at the same time, we must talk to Him with all reverence and respect. It is important to maintain fellowship with God by talking with Him many times each day, for the believer can pray in any place and at any time. God deserves our worship and praise; however, He requires that it to be done with a clean heart and life, so that what we say will be more than just words. The immediate confession of our sins is important so that nothing hinders our fellowship with God. We need to express our love and our thanks to God for all that He has done for us. We should pray to God with sincerity and faith in the name of Jesus Christ. We should not be self-centered in our prayers, but also pray for the spiritual needs of our brethren in Christ. As we pray, we need to include those who have spiritual and civil authority over us. Above all, we must always pray that God's will be done.

I suggest that you maintain a list to help you remember to pray for specific people and their special needs and requests, and later make note of the answers to your prayers. Below there is an example of how it can be done.

Date	Name	Request	The Answer

REVIEW QUESTIONS - CHAPTER 9

THE IMPORTANCE OF PRAYER

1. God wants to have fellowship with all true Christians. Why? _____
   _____

2. Besides our family, for whom should we pray?

   a. _____ b. _____
   c. _____ d. _____
   e. _____ f. _____

3. Does God hear the prayers of everyone? _____ Why? (Psalm 66:18; Isaiah 1:15-20) _____

4. Does God answer our requests because we repeat them often or loudly? _____ Why? (Matthew 6:7) _____
   _____

5. Does God hear the sincere prayers of the sinner, who has a contrite and willing heart to hear God's Word? (Psalm 34:18; Psalm 51:17)_____

6. Where should we pray? _____

7. When should we pray? _____

8. How many times should we pray each day?_____

9. In all of our prayers, we should always pray that the _____ of God be done. (1ˢᵗ John 5:14)

10. We should pray to _____ in the name of_____(John 15:16)

11. Just because we pray in the name of Jesus Christ, does it assure us that we will receive what we request? _____ Why? _____
    _____

12. Is it possible to make a wrong petition to God? _____ Why? (James 4:3) _____
    _____

13. What are some of the conditions God requires in order to have our prayers answered? (John 15:7, 16-17; 1ˢᵗ John 3:22)

    a. _____

    b. _____

    c. _____

14. Who helps us express our needs in prayer? _____

15. Who is our Great High Priest? (Hebrews 10:19-23) _____

16. Give two reasons why it is important to pray every day. _____
    _____
    _____
    _____

17. For which things should we give thanks to God? _____
_____

18. Should we give thanks to God for difficult things that happen to us? Why?
_____ (1st Thessalonians 5:18) _____
_____

19. Why should we worship God in prayer? _____
_____
_____

20. When we pray should we lift our hands into the air so that God can see
our holy hands? _____ What does "lifting up holy hands, without wrath
and doubting," signify? _____
_____
_____

21. Please underline the definition that best explains prayer.
    a. It is repeating a religious ritual.
    b. It is something that is memorized.
    c. It is using a book of prayers.
    d. It is an expression to God with our own words, coming from the
        depth of our heart.

22. We talk to God through _____ and God talks to us through
    the _____ of _____, the Bible.

23. Please memorize Hebrews 4:15-16 and express it in your own words.
_____
_____
_____
_____

In view of the fact that we belong to the Lord Jesus Christ we are God's
property. He has given us many privileges and blessings. With these privileges,
we all have many responsibilities before God. Study Chapter Ten to have a
better understanding of what God's Word instructs us to do as true Christians.

Chapter Ten

The Responsibilities of the True Christian

But ye are a chosen generation, a royal priesthood, an holy nation, a peculiar people; that ye should shew forth the praises of him who hath called you out of darkness into his marvelous light; Which in time past were not a people, but are now the people of God: which had not obtained mercy, but now have obtained mercy.

1st Peter 2:9-10

WE ARE A FAMILY AND GOD IS OUR FATHER.

Ephesians 2:19 declares, *Now therefore ye are no more strangers and foreigners, but fellow citizens with the saints, and of the household of God.* Now that we belong to Christ, we are members of the family of God, and have many new responsibilities to assume. In obedience to the Word of God, it is necessary to associate with those who are members of this spiritual family. Jesus Christ wants us to be united in a group that is referred to as the "local church."

I. GOD ORDAINED THE LOCAL CHURCH.

1. **What does the word, *church* mean?** The word, *church,* is translated from the Greek, ecclesia, or (ek-kaleo) which means, "the called-out ones," or "separated ones." When Jesus Christ stated in Matthew 16:18, *I will build my church,* what did He mean? Jesus Christ builds His church by giving us His faith and bringing us to repentance for salvation. This is the work that only He can do. God has called us out of the world to become members of His family. In Revelation 21:2-3, the Apostle John makes reference to the Church as the "Bride of Christ:" *And I John saw the holy city, new Jerusalem, coming down from God out of Heaven, prepared as a _____ adorned for her husband. And I heard a great voice out of Heaven saying, Behold, the tabernacle of God is with men, and he will dwell with them, and they shall be his people, and God himself shall be with them, and be their God.*

2. **Who is the head of the church?** In Colossians 1:18, the Apostle Paul assures us that Jesus Christ *is the _____ of the body, the church: who is the beginning, the firstborn from the dead; that in all things he might have the preeminence.* We should not be confused by those who deny the fact that the "Body of Christ" is the "Church," and the "Church" is the "Body of Christ." All true believers are members of His "body." When the Lord Jesus Christ comes again for His Church, it will not be for some local church in particular, but for all truly born-again Christians. The Apostle Paul affirms this teaching in 1st Corinthians 12:12: *For as the body is one, and hath many members, and all the members of that one body, being many, are _____ body: so also is Christ.* This is not speaking of a local church, but "one body" that is united in Jesus Christ.

3. **When did Jesus begin to build His Church?** In the beginning of His ministry, Jesus Christ began to build His Church. On the day of Pentecost, when the Apostle Peter and the other apostles preached the salvation message, 3,000 were converted to Jesus Christ. They were saved by God's grace and baptized, as Acts 2:41 affirms: *Then they that gladly received his Word were baptized: and the same day there were _____ unto them about three thousand souls.* The fact that they were "added" to the Body of Christ, indicates that they were not the first. God called this group of true believers into one body, the Church. Throughout all the letters of the Apostles

Paul, Peter, John and Matthew, as well as Luke and James, "the Church of Jesus Christ" is mentioned. The word, church, appears more than one hundred and ten times in the New Testament. The church of the New Testament is not the same as Israel in the Old Testament; however, Romans 4:1-9 affirms that Abraham and David were saved by faith in the same way we have been saved. Also, many other people-of-faith in the Old Testament are mentioned in Hebrews 11. Even though they were not part of the local church of Jesus Christ, they were by faith part of the "Body of Christ." As we look back by faith to that supreme sacrifice of Jesus Christ for our sins on the cross, even so the believers of the Old Testament looked forward by faith to the supreme sacrifice of Jesus Christ for their sins, as the "Lamb of God." We should not be confused, thinking that the true believers of the Old Testament will not participate in the rapture with the believers of the New Testament, when Jesus comes for His "Body." We are one body in Christ Jesus!

4. **What is a local church?** The local church is a congregation of born-again believers, who have repented with all their heart for their sin and deposited their confidence in Jesus Christ as their personal Savior. They are baptized by immersion in water, identifying themselves with Christ and the local church, observing the ordinances of Christ, united and governed by the doctrines of the Word of God, and united in the fellowship of the Gospel. The ministry of the church is to glorify Christ, to teach and help them grow through preaching, teaching, exhortation, worship, prayer, fellowship and personal discipline. The local church has been commissioned in Matthew 28:18-20 and Mark 16:15 to spread the Gospel of Jesus Christ, to baptize and teach those who have been saved. These verses show that we all have a biblical responsibility to give a verbal witness to the lost of the saving and transforming power of Jesus Christ.

5. **Who governs the local church?** The form of governing the local church is "Christocratic," of which Christ Jesus is the Head. The leader of the local church is the bishop. He is referred to as pastor or elder, whose qualifications and duties are found in 1st Timothy 3:1-7, Titus 1:5-9 and 1st Peter 5:1-4. Both the authority and the direction of the local church come from the Word of God, which guides and exhorts in all spiritual truths. The pastor is responsible to the church, and above all to God, for what he is doing in fulfilling

his responsibilities. The material buildings, ministries, and activities are supervised and supported by the members. In the early church the apostles commissioned the members of the church to choose spiritual men for definite responsibilities in the church. We see an example of this mentioned in Acts 6:1-7: *Look* [choose] *ye out among you seven men of honest report, _____ of the Holy Spirit and wisdom, whom we may appoint over this business* [work]. The qualifications for this ministry are given in 1st Timothy 3:8-13. They are referred to as deacons (servants of the church), and are to take an active part by helping the pastor with the members of the church, to oversee and encourage them in their spiritual and physical needs. A key practice for each member is to study the Bible diligently, live in fellowship with God, and to be guided by the Holy Spirit in his life, especially when it comes to participating in the ministry of the church.

The local church is completely independent and autonomous, free of any external authority. The decisions regarding the activities and ministries of the local church are not made by a superintendent, president of an exterior organization, or a convention, but by the members of the local church. The pastor helps to direct the deacons and the church members in the determination of those decisions, which concern the activities of the church. Every member of the church has equal privileges to voice their opinion and can normally vote in the meetings regarding those matters. It is a privilege as well as a great responsibility to help in the decisions that affect the work of the Lord in the local church. However, touching the spiritual areas of doctrine and biblical practices, it is not for the congregation to vote whether or not they will obey God's Word. This is imperative! The Apostle Paul teaches in Ephesians 4:11-12, *And he* (God) *gave some, apostles; and some, prophets; and some, evangelists; and some, pastors and teachers; for the perfecting of the saints, for the work of the ministry, for the _____ of the body of Christ.* God has ordained pastors for the ministry of the Word. The authority and the leadership for the church come from the Word of God and the Holy Spirit.

6. **Who is responsible for the preaching and teaching in the local church?** God has ordained the pastor of the church to care for all the members and also, for those who attend. In 1st Peter 5:2-3, the Apostle Peter confirmed this responsibility: _____ *the flock*

156

of God which is among you, taking the oversight thereof, not by constraint, but willingly; not for filthy lucre, but of a ready mind; Neither as being lords over God's heritage, but being ensamples to the flock. It is necessary that the members have a submissive attitude, as well as a desire to serve the Lord along with the pastor. The Apostle Paul explained in 1st Timothy 3:1-9, the prerequisites for all pastors, which are summarized with the word, "blameless," used in verse 2: *A bishop* [pastor] *then must be blameless, the husband of one wife, vigilant, sober, of good behaviour, given to hospitality, apt to teach.* Hebrews 13:17 shows the importance of obeying the biblical teachings and disciplines given by the pastor of a church: *Obey them* [pastors] *that have the rule over you, and submit yourselves: for they watch for your souls, as they that must give _____, that they may do it with joy, and not with grief: for that is unprofitable for you.* It is important to be in agreement with the teachings, principles and practices of the local church where you are a member.

7. What things characterized the believers of the primitive church?

   Please read Acts 2:41-42 and 47.

   a. They received the _____ (the teachings).

   b. They were _____ . (immersed in water).

   c. They continued in the _____ of the apostles.

   d. They continued in the _____ one with another.

   e. They continued in the breaking of the _____ .

   f. They continued in _____ (talking with God).

   g. They were _____ God (adoration).

II. THE LOCAL CHURCH HAS TWO ORDINANCES.

   a. Baptism is the immersion or submersion in water of the believer in obedience to the command of our Lord Jesus Christ, as taught in Matthew 28:19: *Go ye therefore, and teach all nations, _____ them in the name of the Father, and of the Son, and of the Holy Ghost* [Holy Spirit]. This is an order given by Jesus Christ, it is not an option that a Christian can ignore.

b. When the believer is baptized by immersion in water, he is identified with Christ in His death, burial and resurrection. This act signifies what Christ did for us, by taking our place by receiving our eternal punishment, thereby making possible our salvation. Baptism represents three things – a) **death**, our death to sin, b) **burial** our separation from the former worldly life, and c) **resurrection** our new life in Christ Jesus to serve Him. This is illustrated in Romans 6:5-6: *For if we have been planted together in the likeness of his _____, we shall be also in the likeness of his resurrection: knowing this, that our old man is crucified with him, that the body of sin might be destroyed, that henceforth we should not serve sin.* Read also Galatians 2:20.

Death   Burial   Resurrection

c. Water baptism is also our identification with the local church in its doctrine, principles and practices, projects and ministries. It is also an identification with those who are members of that local church. The Apostle Paul mentioned this at the close of many of his letters by sending greetings to individual members of that local church. Notice the greeting in Colossians 4:15: *Salute the brethren which are in Laodicea, and Nymphas, and the _____ which is in his house.*

d. At times, there is confusion regarding the use of the word, "baptism," as is mentioned in Chapter One. When the Bible mentions **baptism**, it does not necessarily refer to water baptism. This is important to understand! The moment we are saved, we are placed or baptized into the family of God upon believing, depositing our confidence in Christ Jesus and giving ourselves to Him. Acts 2:38 commands, *Repent, and be _____ every one of you in the name of Jesus Christ for the remission* [forgiveness] *of sins, and ye shall receive the gift of the Holy Spirit.* We must understand that this act has nothing to do with water. Repenting of our sins is a personal decision, brought about through the conviction of the Word of God by the Holy Spirit. It is our decision to "put ourselves into" Christ Jesus to become His property. In other words, we give ourselves totally to Jesus Christ for salvation and He makes us members of His family. In Acts 3:19, the Apostle Peter preached another message that was similar to the first, when he gave emphasis to the same subject of salvation. He commanded, *Repent ye therefore, and be converted, that your sins may be blotted out, when the times of refreshing shall come from the presence of the Lord.* There is a slight difference in the wording of these two passages. Acts 2:38 uses the word, "baptism" and Acts 3:19 uses the word, "converted." The only way that sin can be forgiven or "blotted out" is through a true conversion to Jesus Christ, being placed (baptized) into Jesus Christ. Let me emphasize once again that it is not the acceptance of the "gift" of salvation on the part of the lost sinner, but it is the giving of oneself to Jesus Christ in order to receive salvation. That is when God makes the lost sinner a member of His family!

e. Baptism in water does not have any part in salvation, nor does it give us special merits with God, nor can it help us to be more spiritual. It does not wash or take away sins. Baptism in water is a clear testimony of our identification with Christ and the local church. If the believer does not want to be baptized, it is an act of rebellion and is direct disobedience to God. If someone was baptized in obedience to Christ and His command in a church that teaches error, he is associated automatically with error. It is only right that he no longer remains associated with error. It is expedient that he be baptized in water in a church that teaches and preaches sound doctrine, and is faithful to the fundamentals and practices of the Word of God.

2. The Lord's Supper

Jesus Christ initiated the "Lord's Supper" in the presence of His apostles in the upper room the night before His death.

a. The significance of the Lord's Supper is important for the Christian. By participating in the Lord's Supper, we are remembering His horrible death on the cross as He took upon Himself our terrible sins and received in our stead the punishment that we deserved. Jesus declared time and again that He was going to give His body to die on the cross for our sin. In 1st Corinthians 11:23-25, the Apostle Paul explains why the Lord's Supper was instituted for us to commemorate: *For I have received of the Lord that which also I delivered unto you, that the Lord*

159

Jesus the same night in which he was betrayed took bread: And when he had given thanks, he brake it, and said, Take, eat: this [is] my body, which is broken for you: this do in remembrance of me. After the same manner also he took the cup, when he had supped, saying, This cup is the new testament in my blood: this do ye, as oft as ye drink it, in remembrance of me. We always do this in remembrance of His physical death on the cross.

b. There are important truths regarding the elements used in the Lord's Supper.

1) What does the unleavened bread represent? The bread without leaven (yeast) is important because it represents the person of Jesus Christ. In the Bible, leaven always symbolizes corruption, sin and error. Therefore, in the Lord's Supper, bread without yeast is used to represent the personal holiness of the Lord Jesus Christ in all His perfection.

2) What does the cup of grape juice without fermentation represent? The grape juice without fermentation represents the blood of Jesus Christ. In the celebration of the Lord's Supper, grape juice without yeast or fermentation should always be used, because the fresh juice represents the perfection of Christ Jesus without sin. Being God, the Lord Jesus Christ in no way was contaminated by the corruption of our sin or error. 1st Peter 2:24 tells us that Jesus Christ willingly took upon Himself our sins in His own body on the cross. He received upon Himself the judgment of God for our sins when dying on the cross, but at the same time, Jesus Christ maintained all His sinless perfection and holiness.

c. Why should we participate in the Lord's Supper?

1) We should participate in the Lord's Supper, because it is an order given by Jesus Christ in memory of Him. In no way can it bring us some "special grace" or favor. We partake of the Lord's Supper in obedience to His command.

2) They did not eat His body, nor did they drink His blood. The bread and juice was not transformed into the body and blood of Jesus Christ. It is not making a sacrifice once again of the body of Jesus Christ. Those who promote such a teaching

160

are advocating an immense error and it is unbiblical! By participating in this ordinance, it is impossible to receive any "special grace." **We participate in the Lord's Supper only in memory of Him.**

3) When we participate in the Lord's Supper, we are remembering that the Lord Jesus Christ will come again to receive us in the air. The Apostle Paul gave this great teaching in 1st Corinthians 11:26: *For as often as ye eat this bread, and drink this cup, ye do shew the Lord's death till He come.* In 1st Thessalonians 4:13-18, the Bible teaches that the dead in Christ will be resurrected first, and immediately we who are alive will be taken up with them. This is the "blessed hope" of the Christian!

d. How often should we participate in the Lord's Supper? The Bible does not stipulate how often the local church should celebrate the Lord's Supper, but in 1st Corinthians 11:26 it states, *For as often as ye eat this bread, and drink this cup, ye do shew the Lord's death till He come.* The individual local church determines the frequency of their participation in the Lord's Supper.

e. If the church member has unconfessed sin in his life, would it be justifiable for him not to partake of the Lord's Supper? No! Each of us must examine our own heart, confess our sins to God, ask for forgiveness, and then receive the Lord's Supper. It is very important to follow what 1st John 1:9 teaches: *If we _____ our sins, he is faithful and just to forgive us our sins, and to _____ us from all unrighteousness.* In 1st Corinthians 11:27-28, the Apostle Paul admonishes us to examine our heart before we partake of the Lord's Supper: *Wherefore whosoever shall eat this bread, and drink this cup of the Lord, unworthily, shall be guilty of the body and blood of the Lord. But let a man _____ himself, and so let him eat of that bread, and drink of that cup.* What does this mean? Some believe that they cannot receive the Lord's Supper because they do not deserve it or are not good enough to receive it. They fear the possibility of receiving a judgment from God. We obey God, not because we deserve His blessings, but because we love Him. Jesus Christ will never accept any excuse for not getting our life right with Him.

There is only one reason for not partaking of the Lord's Supper. If one has recently been converted, and has not yet been baptized and become a member of a local church, then he should wait until he has been baptized. However, he should be present to pray, asking the Lord to forgive his sin. We must not let Satan rob us of our fellowship with God and other believers.

III. HOW DOES SOMEONE BECOME A MEMBER OF A LOCAL CHURCH?

Each church is an independent entity, responsible to God for its own actions, government and discipline. Each church may have different requirements to become a member of that local church. There are differences in practice, even some differences in doctrines between individual churches. Therefore, it is very important to look for a church that is faithful to the Word of God in the preaching, the teaching, and the practice of sound doctrine. It is also important that they faithfully teach separation from worldly practices. To become a member of a local church, you should express your desire and receive orientation from the pastor of that local church.

1. It is essential that the candidate first be converted.

   It is a mandate from God that the person be converted, as stated in Acts 3:19: *Repent ye therefore, and be _____, that your sins may be blotted out, when the times of refreshing shall come from the presence of the Lord.* It is important for the candidate to show by his life that he truly belongs to Christ and maintains a good testimony. Please read Matthew 10:32; Luke 3:8 and Romans 6:4.

2. The candidate should attend an orientation class.

   Many Bible-believing churches require a time before baptizing the new believer in order to give him an opportunity to receive biblical direction and instruction. This helps him to understand more about Bible doctrine, the principles and practices of the local church. Also, it helps him to understand what his responsibilities will be as a member of the church.

3. The candidate should be baptized.

   It is important for the new believer to be baptized biblically by immersion in water. Baptism in water is a mandate that Jesus Christ gave in Matthew 28:19-20. By baptism we are publicly identifying ourselves with Jesus Christ and with the doctrines of that local church.

162

IV. THE LOCAL CHURCH HAS GOD-GIVEN RESPONSIBILITIES.

The local church has a very important part in the life of the Christian. There are those who have mistaken concepts regarding the local church and the responsibilities of its members.

1. The local church should maintain personal and collective holiness. The most important responsibility of the local church is to maintain its faithfulness to the Word of God and the purity of its members in every aspect of their life. Ephesians 2:19-22 declares, *Now therefore ye are no more strangers and foreigners, but fellow citizens with the saints, and of the household of God; And are built upon the foundation of the apostles and prophets, Jesus Christ himself being the chief corner stone; In whom all the building fitly framed together groweth unto an holy _____ in the Lord: In whom ye also are builded together for an habitation of God through the Spirit.* We are God's holy possession, for we belong to Him and His presence must always be evidenced in our life. 1st Peter 1:15-16 affirms the importance of living a holy life: *But as he which hath called you is holy, so be ye _____ in all manner of conversation* [manner of living]; *Because it is written, Be ye holy; for I am holy.*

2. The local church should give true worship to God. God deserves our worship and praise with a clean heart. Only He is worthy! Worshiping God is comprised of our expressions of adoration in song, in prayer, and by hearing and understanding the truths of the preaching of God's Word. It is essential that we apply these teachings to our daily living. This worship is not a ritual, but a sincere act of adoration in obedience and consecration of ourselves to God. True worship is felt inwardly and then comes out through our daily behavior. God sees through all hypocrisy and He hates worship that is done without a sincere heart. Psalm 95:6-7 declares: *O come, let us _____ and bow down: let us kneel before the Lord our maker. For he is our God; and we are the people of his pasture, and the sheep of his hand.* A powerful example of this is the story of Cain and Abel, the first sons of Adam and Eve. They both brought gift offerings to the Lord, but God was only pleased with Abel's worship. Cain brought a gift of his own choosing, which was not according to God's instructions. Abel brought his finest lamb from his flock for a sacrifice in obedience with true faith and adoration to God.

163

3. It is the pastor's God-given responsibility to preach faithfully the Word of God. The pastor of the local church is not there just to preach a sermon, but he has the responsibility to preach and teach the whole council of the Word of God. The Apostle Paul gave the command to all pastors in 2nd Timothy 4:1-3: *I charge thee therefore before God, and the Lord Jesus Christ, who shall judge the quick and the dead at His appearing and His kingdom; _____ the Gospel; be instant in season, out of season; reprove,* [in Greek the word **reprove** is comprised of two words, "re" and "prove," which actually means – "to prove again or to make a profound investigation"] *rebuke, exhort with all longsuffering* [with patience] *and_____. For the time will come when they will not endure sound doctrine; but after their own lusts* [carnal desires] *shall they heap to themselves teachers, having itching ears.* Unfortunately, in today's world many pastors are trying to please their congregations with their messages, but they do not preach the Word of God with true conviction for the purpose of correcting ungodly sinful living.

The pastor, the deacons and the teachers of a church must obey Titus 2:1 as they carry out their responsibilities: *But speak thou the things which become _____ doctrine.* The Apostle Paul gave the serious order in 2nd Timothy 4:5, *But watch thou in all things, endure afflictions, do the _____ of an evangelist, make full proof of thy ministry.* In Acts 20:28-31, the Apostle Paul lovingly reminded the pastors of Ephesus of the urgent need of caring for the members for whom they were responsible: *Take heed therefore unto yourselves, and to all the flock, over the which the Holy Ghost hath made you _____, to feed the church of God, which he hath purchased with his own blood. For I know this, that after my departing shall grievous wolves enter in among you, not sparing the flock. Also of your own selves shall men arise, speaking perverse things, to draw away disciples after them. Therefore watch, and remember, that by the space of three years I ceased not to warn every one night and day with tears.* Hebrews 13:17 teaches the seriousness of being a pastor. It explains that they will be judged by God as to their faithfulness in their ministries: *Obey them that have the rule over you, and _____ yourselves: for they watch for your souls, as they that must give account, that they may do it with joy, and not with grief: for that is unprofitable for you.* The pastor will give an account to God for all that he does, or does not do in his ministry as also taught in James 3:1.

4. The meetings and services in the local church are for the cultivation of the spiritual growth of the members. It is important that the members faithfully attend the services of the local church. To be absent from these services can only result in the impoverishment of the spiritual life of the Christian. The responsibility of the church is to look for the absentees, call them, visit them, and show concern for them, knowing that when they do not attend the house of God their spiritual life is in jeopardy. In 1st Thessalonians 2:11-14, the Apostle Paul demonstrated his concern for the brethren: *As ye know how we exhorted and comforted and charged every one of you, as a father doth his children, that ye would _____ worthy of God, who hath called you unto his kingdom and glory. For this cause also thank we God without ceasing, because, when ye received the word of God which ye heard of us, ye received it not as the word of men, but as it is in truth, the word of God, which effectually worketh also in you that believe. For ye, brethren, became followers of the churches of God which in Judea are in Christ Jesus.*

5. The local church has the responsibility of protecting the members from attacks of biblical error. This preparation comes through the faithful study of God's Word, which helps them to resist satanic influences. In Ephesians 6:10-18, the Apostle Paul teaches that it is essential for us to be prepared to combat those errors that Satan is always presenting. Ephesians 6:11-13 commands: *Put on the whole armor of God, that ye may be able to _____ against the wiles of the devil. For we wrestle not against flesh and blood, but against principalities, against powers, against the rulers of the darkness of this world, against spiritual wickedness in high places. Wherefore take unto you the whole armor of God, that ye may be able to withstand in the evil day,* [that is every day] *and having done all, to stand.* This is a command for us to stand firm, because Satan desires to discourage us and cause divisions among the brethren. It is crucial for us to faithfully attend church to receive the teaching and preaching from God's Word. In this way we are encouraged and prepared for the battle against Satanic attacks and false doctrines. We are challenged in Hebrews 10:24 to exhort and encourage one another.

6. It is important for the local church to provide orientation classes in basic biblical doctrines for the new believers. This class is vital to doctrinally prepare the new converts to be baptized, and also offer them the opportunity to resolve their doubts. It is the

responsibility of the church to teach and baptize those who are true disciples of Jesus Christ. Matthew 28:19 says, *Go ye therefore, and _____ all nations, baptizing them in the name of the Father, and of the Son, and of the Holy Spirit: teaching them to observe all things whatsoever I have commanded you: and, lo, I am with you alway, even unto the end of the world. Amen.*

7. The local church has the responsibility to serve the Lord's Supper to the members of the church in obedience to the Word of God. The Apostle Paul shares, in 1st Corinthians 11:26, the instructions that he received from the Lord Jesus Christ: *For as often as ye eat this bread, and drink this cup, ye do shew the Lord's death till He come.* Verse 24 commands, *This do in remembrance of me.* We must never forget what Christ did for us when He died on the cross and arose from the dead.

8. The local church has the responsibility to encourage the members to pray together for the church and its activities. They should pray especially for the workers of the church, the pastor, the deacons (servants) and the teachers. They should pray for the regular worship services, Sunday School, for the spiritual growth of the different ministries of the church, its programs and projects. They should pray for the missionaries, especially for those who are supported by that local church. The Apostle Paul requested prayer for his missionary work in Ephesians 6:18-20: *Praying always with all prayer and supplication in the Spirit, and watching thereunto with all perseverance and supplication for all saints; and for me, that utterance may be given unto me, that I may open my _____ boldly, to make known the mystery of the gospel, for which I am an ambassador in bonds: that therein I may speak boldly, as I ought to speak.*

9. The local church should give responsibilities to its faithful members. Each member is responsible before God to be faithful administrators of his life, talents, possessions, money and time. 1st Corinthians 4:2 emphasizes faithfulness: *It is required in stewards, that a man be found _____.* God requires us to be faithful administrators in everything.

10. The local church must always maintain discipline and reverence in the services and meetings. The brethren must be taught the importance of maintaining order in the church. We are taught in Habakkuk 2:20, *But the Lord is in his holy temple: let all the earth*

keep _____ *before him.* Teach your children how they should behave in God's house by showing respect, love and honor to God. They must sit quietly, pay attention to God's Word being preached, and take notes of what the pastor is saying. The Bible clearly teaches that the women must keep silent in the church as commanded in 1st Timothy 2:11-12. Both men and women should realize that when they speak out loudly in the service, saying "Amen," it draws attention to themselves, and many will turn to see who is talking. This is a distraction from the message, and can often cause others to be disorderly and miss the important teaching of God's Word. All disorder dishonors God! In 1st Corinthians 14:40, the Apostle Paul insisted, *Let all things be done decently and in* _____. As we practice order and discipline in our homes and other areas of our life, a greater respect and honor for God will overflow into the church.

11. The local church has the responsibility to evangelize those who do not know the Lord Jesus Christ as their Savior. The emphasis on visitation is important. The church should have a visitation program with as many members as possible participating. Besides having organized visitation, each believer should share his testimony with unsaved family members, neighbors, classmates, coworkers, and everywhere God gives him the opportunity to evangelize. 1st Peter 3:15 teaches, *But sanctify* [live holy lives] *the Lord God in your hearts: and be ready always to give an* _____ *to every man that asketh you a reason of the hope that is in you with meekness and fear.*

Many church members set aside one hour each week to give a Bible class to an unsaved person, using the book, ***Becoming a True Christian***. I want to encourage you to consider this type of ministry. These home Bible study classes result in the salvation of many people and are also a great spiritual encouragement to fellow believers. The responsibility of every Christian is to teach the Word of God to those who are not saved, take them to church and lead them to the Lord. The Lord Jesus Christ gave the order in Matthew 28:19-20, *Go ye therefore, and* _____ *all nations, baptizing them in the name of the Father, and of the Son, and of the Holy Ghost: teaching them to observe all things whatsoever I have commanded you: and, lo, I am with you alway, even unto the end of the world. Amen.* The ministry of making disciples is not only to teach Christians more of God's Word, but also to reach unsaved people through the teaching of God's Word. It is of utmost importance that they understand and come to a true conversion to Jesus Christ, and continue to receive discipleship classes after their conversion. In Philippians 2:15, the Apostle Paul teaches us to be *blameless and harmless, the sons of God, without rebuke, in the midst of a crooked and perverse nation, among whom ye shine as* _____ *in the world.* If we are obedient to Christ, He will richly bless us.

V. WE MUST PROTECT THE LOCAL CHURCH FROM WORLDLY MUSIC.

1. The local church needs to reject worldly music styles. The entrance of Contemporary Christian music has brought great confusion into our churches. The fact that Contemporary Christian music is popular does not make it right. Music is not amoral or neutral. Many of todays generation deny the fact of the powerful influence of music. Music is a moral vehicle that has the power to provoke and to influence us to do good or evil depending on its style, composition and how it is performed. Worldly music cannot deliver a moral message that would glorify our holy God. Many church leaders deny the powerful influences of the rhythm of Contemporary Christian music. Some accept all forms of music suggesting that it does not matter to God what types of music they listen to in their homes or use in their churches. They give no true biblical basis for using Contemporary Christian music, but only offer their desires and opinions. Often times they twist the meaning of 1st Corinthians 9:22 to infer that their music is reaching the unsaved: *To the weak became I as weak, that I might gain the weak: I am made all things to all men, that I might by* _____ *means save some.* Isaiah 5:20 warns, *Woe unto them that call evil good, and good evil; that put darkness for light, and light for darkness; that put bitter for sweet, and sweet for bitter!* They are revealing incorrect attitudes and their profound love for the world.

2. Music has been the subject of debate throughout history, especially as it relates to worship. This issue has been aggravated by continued exposure to subtle, and not so subtle, forms of music that have made inroads into the churches. By adding to this mixture a multitude of backgrounds and experiences, the result is a broad range of acquired musical tastes. Many consider themselves an authority on this subject, proclaiming that their styles are the most appropriate for

their spiritual needs. We must defend biblical truths, and practice Scriptural principles that reveal godly music for the ministry of the church. The purpose of music in the church is not to entertain, nor to attract prospective members, even though many churches accept music on these terms. In order to accomplish these current trends, many ministries have chosen to use styles of music that are worldly. We do not question the sincerity of anyone, but our music should honor and glorify God as commanded in Colossians 3:16: *Let the Word of Christ dwell in you richly in all wisdom; teaching and admonishing one another in psalms and hymns and spiritual songs, singing with grace in your hearts to the Lord.* **Is your music spiritual, edifying the brethren, and testifying to the holiness, love and power of God?** Those who are using contemporary music are imitating the world and are missing the blessing of singing majestic, harmonious music with grace in your hearts to the Lord.

3. The general movement of Contemporary Christian music attempts to carry a moral message that appeals to the spirit, using an immoral vehicle of music that appeals to the flesh. The one corrupts the other, and thus hinders the spiritual growth of the believer. The repetitive savage rhythm, accompanied with applauding, lifts the emotions and incites sensual movements of the body. Its origin is clearly from the world and consequently worldly. *Worldly* simply means – "something of the world, or like the world." In 2nd Corinthians 4:4, Satan is called the god of this world. One of Satan's goals is to blind the minds and hearts of those who do not understand nor receive the truth of God's Word. Satan wants to introduce modern and worldly music into the church for the purpose of driving a wedge inside the church, which causes division among its members. The Apostle Paul admonishes us in 1st Corinthians 1:10, *Now I beseech you, brethren, by the name of our Lord Jesus Christ, that ye all speak the same thing* [be in agreement]*, and that there be no* _____ *among you; but that ye be perfectly joined together in the same mind and in the same judgment.* Worldly music provokes sensuality, which comes from a sinful life. Such music does not glorify God! God rejects it as He proclaims in Amos 5:23-24: *Take thou away from me the noise of thy songs; for I will not hear the melody of thy viols* [instruments]*. But let judgment run down as waters, and righteousness as a mighty stream.* Contemporary Christian music comes by attributing "Christian" words to worldly music. This can never honor the Lord in our worship services. When you apply the

beat or worldly rhythms to a Gospel hymn it causes us to loss the message.

4. The Christian is to be different from the world. The music that you desire reflects what you believe concerning God. We should please God the Father by maintaining a consecrated life to Christ, because we belong to Him. In John 17:16-17, Jesus prayed for His followers in this way: *They are not of the world, even as I am not of the world. Sanctify* [set apart] *them through thy truth: thy word is truth.* The Apostle Paul declared in 1st Corinthians 1:18, *For the preaching of the cross is to them that perish foolishness; but unto us which are saved it is the power of God.* One method that modern Christendom is using to make the church attractive to the world is through Contemporary Christian music. Because of this fellowship, fusion or union with the world, there is confusion and a growing ignorance of the teachings of the Word of God regarding the believer's separation from physical, emotional and spiritual worldliness. In 2nd Corinthians 6:14-18 God commands that there be a definite difference between the worldly life and the life of the true Christian. Ephesians 5:10 tells us that we should be *proving what is acceptable unto the Lord.* We should maintain traditional and not controversial new worldly musical styles in our services. Our church music should reflect the majesty and peace of God. Philippians 4:8 has a list we should follow in every area of our life: *Finally, brethren, whatsoever things are true, whatsoever things are honest, whatsoever things are just, whatsoever things are pure, whatsoever things are lovely, whatsoever things are of good report; if there be any virtue, and if there be any praise, think on these things.* There is a great necessity to align our thoughts and actions with the purity and holiness of God. We must reflect the authority of God in our life in all we are, have and do. Those that live this way will truly honor and glorify our heavenly Father.

5. We have an all-powerful God, who wants to be adored and praised with reverent and majestic music. We must not permit worldly music in the church of the Lord Jesus Christ. There is a great need to stand firm on these convictions, first in our homes, for that is where our appetites for good music are developed. This will help maintain godly music in the church. Jude 1:3-4 gives this warning: *Beloved, when I gave all diligence to write unto you of the common salvation, it was needful for me to write unto you, and exhort you*

that ye should earnestly _____ for the faith which was once delivered unto the saints. For there are certain men crept in unawares, who were before of old ordained to this condemnation, ungodly men, turning the grace of our God into lasciviousness, and denying the only Lord God, and our Lord Jesus Christ. Satan wants to erode the effectiveness of the local church from the inside out for the purpose of destroying it. Even though some churches use majestic traditional Christian music in the church services, why is Contemporary Christian music being tolerated in many of the children's classes and youth groups? What are they teaching to their children? Why are the youth leaders permitted to use this music? Also, there is often another conflict, because worldly music is being allowed in the home! There is no place for worldly music in the life and home of the true Christian. We should not allow the rebellion and scorn of the world destroy the church.

6. In Titus 2:11-15 the Apostle Paul teaches the necessity of renouncing ungodliness and worldly desires: *For the grace of God that bringeth salvation hath appeared to all men, teaching us that, denying ungodliness and worldly lusts, we should live soberly, righteously, and godly, in this present world; looking for that blessed hope, and the glorious appearing of the great God and our Savior Jesus Christ; who gave himself for us, that he might redeem us from all iniquity, and purify unto himself a peculiar* [unique] *people, zealous of good works. These things speak, and exhort, and _____ with all authority. Let no man despise thee.* There are those who believe that Contemporary Christian music must be used if we are to reach the lost. The evangelization of the lost is a ministry to be fulfilled by each member of the church. We should not use ungodly vehicles (methods or people) to reach ungodly people for the Lord. There is no biblical support for that type of evangelism. If we want to see a person's life changed, we must not use those elements that contribute to his current lost condition. Christ has given the true believer a new song, which is not of the world. Psalm 96:1-4 declares, *O sing unto the Lord a new song: sing unto the Lord, all the earth. Sing unto the Lord, bless his name; shew forth his salvation from day to day. Declare his glory among the heathen, his wonders among all people. For the Lord is great, and greatly to be praised: he is to be feared above all gods.* When we belong to the Lord Jesus Christ, He truly gives us a new song.

VI. EVERY MEMBER OF THE LOCAL CHURCH HAS RESPONSIBILITIES.

There are many members who ignore the biblical teachings and the commitment they have made to support the purposes of the local church in all its functions; consequently, they are rejecting their God-given responsibilities. Each member is important to the function of the local church.

1. Each member of the local church should faithfully attend the services and meetings of the church to hear the teaching and preaching of the Word of God Sunday morning, Sunday evening and during the week. Hebrews 10:23-26 gives important instructions for our spiritual growth: *Let us hold fast the profession of our faith without wavering; (for He is faithful that promised;) And let us consider one another to provoke unto love and to good works: Not _____ the assembling of ourselves together, as the manner of some is; but exhorting one another: and so much the more, as ye see the day approaching. For if we sin willfully after that we have received the knowledge of the truth, there remaineth no more sacrifice for sins.* This admonishes us to be faithful in our church attendance. The Christian should set aside the Lord's Day to worship God and receive the teachings from God's Word to enable him to grow in the Lord and to prepare to serve God better. When a person no longer attends church, he is disobeying God. There is no other solution but to repent and return to church with a changed attitude, determined to be faithful to Jesus Christ.

2. The members of the local church should love one another, encourage one another, and protect one another against the attacks of error. Have you shown concern for other members, visiting or calling those who are not attending? It is possible they are experiencing discouraging times. It is necessary to visit the sick and shut-ins. In John 13:34-35, the Lord Jesus Christ commands us to love all true Christians as He loves us: *A new commandment I give unto you, that ye _____ one another; as I have loved you, that ye also love one another. By this shall all men know that ye are my disciples, if ye have _____ one to another.*

3. Another personal responsibility of the church member is to cultivate spiritual growth among the brethren. We must encourage one another to be obedient to the Word of God. It is essential to keep

peace and unity among the brethren, avoiding conflicts by shunning gossip and criticism. If a conflict exists among the brethren, it should to be resolved as soon as possible. In Matthew 5:23-24, Jesus Christ cautioned the believers: *Therefore if thou bring thy gift to the altar, and there rememberest that thy brother hath ought against thee; leave there thy gift before the altar, and go thy way; first be _____ to thy brother, and then come and offer thy gift.* We need to get the conflicts resolved, remembering that the Lord has called us to peace and love. In Romans 12:1, God calls us to a holy life: *I beseech you therefore, brethren, by the mercies of God, that ye present your _____ a living sacrifice, holy, acceptable unto God, which is your reasonable service.* We should daily present our bodies as a sacrifice to God.

4. The members should pray for each other, for their pastor, for their leaders and for the brethren of the church and their activities. In 2nd Thessalonians 3:1, the Apostle Paul requests, *Finally, brethren, _____ for us, that the word of the Lord may have free course, and be glorified, even as it is with you.* It is important to attend the prayer meetings in the church, to hear and pray for the petitions that each person has on his heart, and not miss the blessings of hearing God's Word taught. We should take time every day to enjoy reading the Word of God and to pray in private and also with the family.

5. All the members should participate in the support of the church. When we are faithful to Christ, we will fulfill the responsibility of giving our tithes and offerings to the church. We are participating in the support of the work and ministries of the church. These ministries include the management and function of the buildings, the support of the pastor, the promotion of missions, the support of missionaries and evangelism in general. The only way to maintain these ministries is through the tithes and offerings of the brethren. Jesus said in Mark 12:17, *Render to Caesar the things that are Caesar's, and to God the things that are God's.* With joy in our hearts, we give our tithe and offerings to God as He has prospered us each week. The Apostle Paul taught in 1st Corinthians 16:2 a systematic way of tithing and giving: *Upon the first day of the week let every one of you lay by him in _____, as God hath prospered him, that there be no gatherings when I come.* It requires discipline to set aside our tithe as an act of worship and love for Christ. We have to remember that it is our church, and it is our responsibility

to care for it, and to support its physical and spiritual growth.

In 2nd Corinthians 9:5-8, the Apostle Paul gave an important teaching regarding our offerings. The focus is on verse 7: *Every man according as he purposed in his heart, so let him give; not grudgingly, or of necessity: for God loveth a cheerful giver.* According to Matthew 6:21, our giving is an example of our love to God: *For where your treasure is, there will your _____ be also.* God does not want us to be thieves! Malachi 3:8 asks the question, *Will a man _____ God? Yet ye have robbed me. But ye say, Wherein have we robbed thee? In tithes and offerings.* Malachi 3:10 gives the solution: *Bring ye all the tithes into the storehouse* [your local church], *that there may be meat in mine house, and prove me now herewith, saith the Lord of hosts, if I will not open you the windows of Heaven, and pour you out a blessing, that there shall not be room enough to receive it.* In this passage, God is not promising material wealth for us, but His rich blessings and provisions for our necessities. The Scripture is filled with promises that God will honor us if we honor Him.

6. We should ask God for opportunities to serve Him in the local church. All the members of the local church should be willing to accept and faithfully fulfill their responsibilities and positions. It is important for the progress of the work of Christ. 1st Peter 4:10 teaches us, *As every man hath received the gift, even so minister the same one to _____, as good stewards of the manifold grace of God.*

7. All the members of the local church have the privilege and the responsibility to evangelize the world with the Word of God. One way that everyone can evangelize is to visit their neighbors from house to house, offering them a Bible class. We recommend that you set aside one hour each week to have a Bible class with an unsaved person, using the book, *Becoming a True Christian.* These home Bible studies have resulted in the salvation of many people and are also a great spiritual encouragement to fellow believers as they become active in the church. Jesus Christ commands us in Mark 16:15, *Go ye into all the world, and preach* [teach] *the gospel to every creature.* The ministry of making disciples is not only the act of teaching someone, but bringing them to a true conversion to Jesus Christ. I want to encourage you to consider this type of ministry for yourself.

8. Besides reaching souls for Jesus Christ, we should disciple the new believers and encourage them to overcome conflicts and problems in their life. The Apostle Paul gives meaningful counsel in 2ndTimothy 2:1-2, *Thou therefore, my son, be strong in the grace that is in Christ Jesus. And the things that thou hast heard of me among many witnesses, the same commit thou to _____ men, who shall be able to teach others also.* Be faithful!

VII. JESUS CHRIST IS COMING AGAIN!

1. In Titus 2:11-14, the Apostle Paul teaches regarding the "blessed hope" of the true Christian: *For the grace of God that bringeth salvation hath appeared to all men, teaching us that, denying ungodliness and worldly lusts, we should live soberly* [seriously], *righteously, and godly, in this present world; looking for that **blessed hope**, and the glorious _____ of the great God and our Savior Jesus Christ; Who gave himself for us, that he might redeem us from all iniquity, and purify unto himself a peculiar people, zealous of good works.* When the Apostle Paul used the word, **hope**, it is referring to a sure, confident and certain event. Jesus Christ **for sure** will come again for us! In John 14:1-3, Jesus Christ taught His apostles, with all clarity, regarding His return to this earth for us: *Let not your heart be troubled: ye believe in God, believe also in me. In my Father's house are many mansions: if it were not so, I would have told you. I go to prepare a place for _____. And if I go and prepare a place for you, I will come again, and receive you unto myself; that where I am, there ye may be also.*

2. What happens when the believer dies? It is important to understand that the soul and spirit are not sleeping, but go immediately upon death to be with Jesus Christ. The Apostle Paul teaches in 2nd Corinthians 5:6-8, *Therefore we are always confident, knowing that, whilst we are at home in the body, we are absent from the Lord: (For we walk by faith, not by sight:) We are confident, I say, and willing rather to be absent from the body, and to be _____ with the Lord.* The body goes to the grave while waiting for that physical resurrection. 1st Corinthians 15:51-53 explains the change that will happen to the body: *behold, I shew you a mystery; We shall not all sleep, but we shall all be changed, in a moment, in the twinkling of an eye, at the last trump: for the trumpet shall sound, and the dead shall be raised incorruptible, and we shall be _____. For*

this corruptible must put on incorruption, and this mortal must put on immortality. We will have a body transformed with the same qualities as the body of our Lord Jesus Christ when He arose from the dead; however, each individual will have his own personal characteristics as they were known here on the earth. The Apostle John explains this in 1st John 3:2: *Beloved, now are we the sons of God, and it doth not yet appear what we shall be: but we know that, when he shall appear, we shall be like him; for we shall see him as he is.* The Apostle Paul explains more regarding this wonderful coming event in 1st Thessalonians 4:13-18: *But I would not have you to be ignorant, brethren, concerning them which are asleep* [dead], *that ye sorrow not, even as others which have no hope. For if we believe that Jesus died and rose again, even so them also which sleep in Jesus will God bring with him. For this we say unto you by the word of the Lord, that we which are alive and remain unto the coming of the Lord shall not prevent* [precede] *them which are asleep. For the Lord himself shall descend from Heaven with a shout, with the voice of the archangel, and with the trump of God: and the dead in Christ shall _____ first: Then we which are alive and remain shall be caught up _____ with them in the clouds, to meet the Lord in the air: and so shall we ever be with the Lord. Wherefore comfort one another with these words.* In the moment of this glorious event of the coming of Christ Jesus in the air, all true believers will be raised from the dead, and those of us who are alive will be taken physically to be with Him forever. This "blessed hope" is often referred to as the rapture of the believer.

3. In view of the soon return of the Lord, 1st John 3:3 teaches us how we should live: *And every man that hath this hope in him purifieth himself, even as he is pure.* In conclusion, Jude 1:24-25 proclaims, *Now unto him that is able to keep you from falling, and to present you faultless before the presence of his glory with exceeding joy, to the only wise God our Savior, be glory and majesty, dominion and power, both now and ever. Amen.* Won't it be wonderful when we all meet together with our Lord and Savior Jesus Christ in Heaven? I look forward to meeting you there!

Even so, come, Lord Jesus. The grace of our Lord Jesus Christ be with you all. Amen!
Revelation 22:21-22

176

TO THE STUDENT

I trust that this study of God's Word has been a blessing to you, and that this book has been a useful guide in your life. The principal purpose of this book is to help you evangelize those who do not know the Lord Jesus Christ as their Savior and to buildup the true Christian in the faith. If this book has been used by God to help you give your life to Christ, to God be the honor and glory! I would love to hear from you and have you share your testimony with me, so that I can pray for you!

If you have any doubts or questions, please write to me. Be sure to send your complete address. Please express your questions as clearly as possible. This will help me provide you with an adequate answer.

And the very God of peace sanctify you wholly;
and I pray God your whole spirit and soul and body
be preserved blameless unto the coming
of our Lord Jesus Christ.
Faithful is He that calleth you,
who also will do it.

1st Thessalonians 5:23-24

May God richly bless you!

Myron L. Philippi
Pastor Myron L. Philippi

ANSWERS TO REVIEW QUESTIONS

Chapter 1. Page 9 - 11

1. No. Many do not understand the true Gospel.
2. No. Jesus said that He never knew them.
3. No. Even the devils believe.
4. No. No religion can save anyone.
5. Yes. The Bible tells us that we can have this assurance in 1st John 5:13
6. Yes. The Bible shows us exactly how to be saved.
7. No. Salvation is not by works.
8. No. It is not by giving our money or possessions that can save us.
9. No. Salvation cannot be achieved by being faithful to a church.
10. No. Baptism cannot save anyone. Ephesians 2:8-9
11. No. Matthew 7:21-23
12. No. True biblical faith only comes from God.
13. No. Jesus is the only way to God.
14. No. Many are sincere, but sincerely wrong.
15. Yes, He was taught by Gamaliel.
16. No, he hated and persecuted the Christians.
17. Yes. He was very religious.
18. No. Titus 3:5
19. No. Jesus told him where to go to hear the message of salvation.
20. No. Experiences cannot save us.
21. No. It means to place something within or into.
22. Yes. His life was transformed.
23. No. James 2:19, The devils also believe, but are not saved.
24. No. Reforms can bring changes to a life, but not salvation.
25. Yes. John 10:27 – God knows those who are His children. We hear God's Word and will faithfully follow Jesus Christ.

Chapter 2. Page 31 - 32

1. Sin
2. No
3. The justice and holiness of God does not allow Him to overlook our sin. Our sins have to be punished.
4. Yes. Christ came for those who realize they are lost sinners.
5. Yes. There is no salvation without repentance. Romans 2:5
6. No. Ephesians 2:8-9
7. No. Ephesians 2:8-9
8. No. Those who do not realize their terribly lost condition can never receive help from God.
9. Yes, We battle against sin as long as we live. Eph. 6:11-17
10. False
11. True
12. False
13. True
14. True
15. False
16. False
17. True
18. True
19. True
20. True
21. False

Chapter 3. Page 38 - 39
1. Yes
2. Yes
3. Yes
4. No
5. Yes
6. No
7. No
8. Yes
9. Yes
10. Yes
11. No
12. Yes, Yes

Chapter 4. Page 51 - 52
1. False
2. False
3. True
4. True
5. True
6. True
7. False
8. True
9. False
10. True
11. False
12. False
13. True
14. True
15. True
16. False
17. False

Chapter 5. Page 76
1. Answer personally.
2. To have eternal life and to have fellowship with God.
3. By dying on the cross to save us. Rom. 5:8
4. By faith, repenting of my sin and giving myself to Jesus Christ. Ephesians 2:8-9
5. Yes. Without repentance there is no salvation.
6. No
7. Yes. 2nd Timothy 3:12
8. Answer personally.
9. Answer personally.
10. Answer personally.
11. Answer personally.

Chapter 6. Page 97 - 99
1. Yes. To receive our punishment, to forgive our sins and reconcile us to God.
2. Answer personally.
3. God's Word gives us complete assurance. Answer personally.
4. 2nd Timothy 1:12, and many more.
5. Yes, Yes, I am a member of the Family of God. Please answer personally.
6. A "saint" is one who is born again, who is separated from the world for the use of God.
7. Once, all
8. Yes, We still have a sin nature. 1st John 1:8-10
9. Nothing
10. Nothing
11. Unconfessed sin and neglect in our spiritual life.
12. None
13. Only one time
14. No, none
15. No
16. None
17. No
18. Without the shedding of blood there is no forgiveness for sin.
19. Confess his sin, and forsake them.
20. God will discipline him.

21. Discipline is applied to the sinning Christian for the purpose of bringing him under conviction, so that he will confess it and forsake it, thus bringing him back into fellowship with Jesus Christ.

22. All those who are truly born again! Our Lord and Savior Jesus Christ.

23. To give those who belong to Him eternal life, and they shall never perish.

24. No one is able to pluck [take] them out of my Father's hand.

25. We will give an account for those things that we have done, "Good" and "Bad" which have not been confessed.

26. No! Romans 8:1 No, He can never be lost.

Chapter 7. Page 123 - 124

1. The Bible, God's Word
2. No one, the Apostle John included himself.
3. Yes, We are combating the world, the flesh and the devil as long as we live in the world.
4. Love, joy, peace, patience, gentleness, goodness, faithfulness, meekness, and temperance given by the Holy Spirit.
5. The world, the flesh, the devil
6. We ask God for help, submit to Him, be prepared, put on the armor of God's Word, watch and pray, resist the devil, hide God's Word in our heart and repent of our sins.
7. Prayer and Bible study
8. The spiritual battles never end;

however, God gives us continued victories.

9. We belong only to the Lord Jesus Christ and we should be faithful to live for Him and only represent Him. 2nd Cor. 6:14-18

10. Those things are not biblical and they are in opposition to God.

11. Repent and correct yourself. Apply the Word of God to your life! Phil. 4:8-9

12. The Holy Spirit, Romans 8:11, 16; 1st Corinthians 3:16; 1st John 4:13

13. See pages 121 - 122

Chapter 8. Page 135 - 136

1. Holy Spirit.
2. Approximately 39
3. Jesus Christ
4. True
5. False
6. True
7. False
8. Jesus Christ, Jesus Christ
9. See page 130
10. See page 130
11. Doctrine,
    Reproof,
    Correction,
    Instruction,
    Maturity
12. Hear the Word.
    Read the Word.
    Study the Word.
    Meditate on the Word
    Memorize the Word
    Obey the Word
    Teach the Word of God to others

Chapter 9. Page 150 - 152

1. We belong to Jesus Christ, He loves us, we love Him.
2. a. For ourselves, family and friends,
   b. For the unsaved
   c. For brethren in the faith.
   d. For the sick,
   e. For ministers, missionaries, and Christian workers
   f. For government authorities
3. No
4. No
5. Yes
6. Anywhere
7. Anytime
8. Many, We are not limited!
9. Will of God be done
10. God the Father, – Jesus Christ
11. No, It is not a secret password.
12. Yes, Because of wrong attitudes, wrong desires, wrong intentions.
13. See pages 140 – 142
14. The Holy Spirit
15. Jesus Christ
16. To maintain a clean life, and to maintain fellowship with God.
17. Everything, the good and bad
18. Yes, It is God's will.
19. He is worthy of our honor and worship. He desires to hear our expressions of love for Him.
20. No. It is speaking symbolically to help us realize that God sees the sin that we have committed. God insists that we recognize the sin in our life, repent and confess it to Him.
21. It is an expression to God with our own words, coming from the depth of our heart.
22. Prayer – The Word of God

Definitions of terms from page 42 having to do with intellectualism, which are all philosophies of men.

Existentialism, = "A philosophical and literary movement, variously religious and atheistic. It is based on the doctrine that concrete, individual existence takes precedence over abstract, conceptual essence and holds that human beings are totally free and responsible for their acts and that this responsibility is the source of their feelings of dread and anguish."

Metaphysics, = "The branch of philosophy that deals with first principles and seeks to explain the nature of being or reality (ontology) and of the origin and structure of the universe (cosmology): it is closely associated with the study of the nature of knowledge (epistemology), speculative philosophy in general, esoteric, often mystical or theosophical, lore, the theory or principles (of some branch of knowledge), popularly, any very subtle or difficult reasoning."

Mind control, = "This is known as brainwashing, coercive persuasion, mind abuse, menticide, thought control, or thought reform. It refers to a process in which a group or individual "systematically uses unethically manipulative methods to persuade others to conform to the wishes of the manipulator(s), often to the detriment of the person being manipulated" The term has been applied to any tactic, psychological or otherwise, which can be seen as subverting an individual's sense of control over their own thinking, behavior, emotions or decision making. Theories of brainwashing and of mind control were originally developed to explain how totalitarian regimes appeared to succeed systematically in indoctrinating prisoners of war through propaganda and torture techniques. These theories were later expanded and modified by psychologists to explain a wider range of phenomena, especially conversions to new religious movements."

Scientology, = "This teaches that people are immortal beings who have forgotten their true nature. Its method of spiritual rehabilitation is a type of counseling known as auditing, in which practitioners aim to consciously re-experience painful or traumatic events in their past in order to free themselves of their limiting effects. The Church of Scientology is one of the most controversial new religious movements to have arisen in the 20th century. It has often been described as a cult that financially defrauds and abuses its members, charging exorbitant fees for its spiritual services. Further controversy has focused on Scientology's belief that souls ("thetans") reincarnate and have lived on other planets before living on Earth, and that some of the related teachings are not revealed to practitioners until they have paid thousands of dollars to the Church of Scientology."

Cybernetics, = "The control and communication in all of their manifestations within and between machines, animals, and organizations. It is specifically, the interaction between automatic control and living organisms, especially humans and animals."

About the Author

Anne Barab is a Business Consultant who helps people become more resilient by laughing about the tough stuff. She is the former Chief Operating Officer of a $1.5 billion mortgage bank, a three-term recovering politician and a 43 year veteran of the marriage wars. But her greatest claim to fame is raising three adult tax-paying children who've spawned four of the cutest grandkids ever and being voted Best Smelling Mom by her son's first grade class.

Book her to speak at your next event.

OR

Download a recording of her signature keynote titled:

I Had a Life Plan but the Magnet Fell off the Fridge

Go to www.AnneBarab.com

Enter code: LAUGHTOHEAL